Alexander Lukashenko: A Historical Analysis of Europe's Longest Ruling Dictator

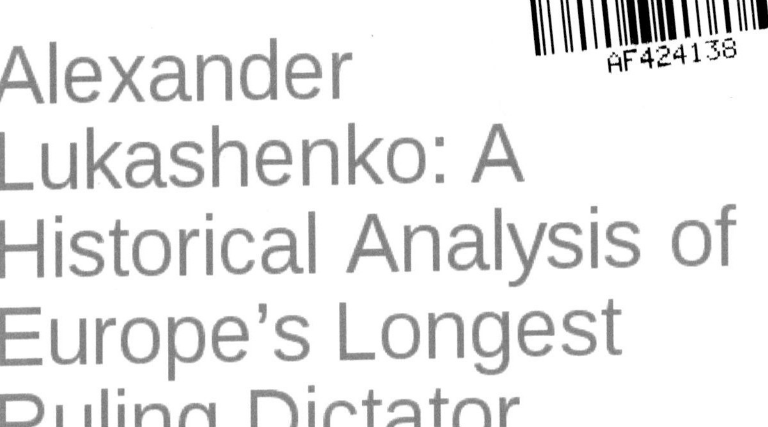

Copyright Page

TITLE: Alexander Lukashenko: A Historical Analysis of Europe's Longest Ruling Dictator

1ST Edition

Copyright @ 2023

Roberto M. Rodriguez. All rights reserved.

ISBN: 9798223296829

Table of Contents

Alexander Lukashenko: A Historical Analysis of Europe's Longest Ruling Dictator

By Roberto Miguel Rodriguez

Chapter 1: Alexander Lukashenko: Europe's Longest Ruling Dictator

Introduction to Alexander Lukashenko's rise to power

Alexander Lukashenko's rise to power marked a significant milestone in the history of Belarus. As historians, it is crucial to delve into the intricacies of his political journey and understand the factors that contributed to his enduring grip on power, making him Europe's longest-ruling dictator. This subchapter aims to provide a comprehensive overview of Lukashenko's rise to power, shedding light on the events and circumstances that shaped his political career.

Lukashenko's ascent to power began in 1994 when he won the presidential elections, promising to bring stability and prosperity to Belarus. His populist appeal, rooted in his promises to revitalize the economy and restore Belarusian nationalism, struck a chord with the disillusioned masses. However, as time progressed, it became evident that Lukashenko's vision for Belarus was far from democratic.

One of the defining characteristics of Lukashenko's rule was his economic policies. The subchapter will explore the impact of these policies on Belarus, examining their long-term consequences for the country's economic stability and development. Lukashenko's heavy-handed approach to economic management, characterized by state control and suppression of private enterprise, had significant implications for the Belarusian people.

Furthermore, Lukashenko's regime was marked by the suppression of political dissent, a topic that warrants comprehensive analysis. The subchapter will delve into the mechanisms employed by Lukashenko to stifle opposition voices, including the manipulation of electoral processes, imprisonment of political opponents, and censorship of independent media. The human rights violations under his regime will be explored, revealing the extent of the authoritarian practices that have plagued Belarus for decades.

Lukashenko's relationship with Russia and its implications for Belarus is another crucial aspect of his rule. The subchapter will analyze the dynamics of this relationship, examining how Lukashenko's alignment with Russia has influenced Belarus' foreign policy and its relations with the European Union and neighboring countries.

In addition, the control exerted by Lukashenko over the media and freedom of speech in Belarus will be thoroughly examined. By exploring the restrictions imposed on journalists and the suppression of dissenting voices, the subchapter will shed light on the manipulation and propaganda machinery employed by Lukashenko to maintain his grip on power.

Lastly, the subchapter will touch upon the Belarusian opposition movements and their tireless struggle against Lukashenko's rule. It will highlight the challenges faced by these movements, their resilience, and the impact of their activism on Belarusian society.

To fully understand Lukashenko's dictatorship, it is vital to examine the international response to his rule. The subchapter will explore the diplomatic efforts, sanctions, and international pressure exerted to address the human rights violations and democratic deficits under Lukashenko's regime.

To conclude, this subchapter sets the stage for a comprehensive analysis of Alexander Lukashenko's rule, shedding light on the various aspects that have characterized his tenure. By examining his rise to power, economic policies, suppression of dissent, human rights violations, relationship with Russia, control over the media, opposition movements, international response, influence on Belarusian culture, and foreign policy, historians can gain a holistic understanding of Europe's longest-ruling dictator and the multifaceted impact of his rule on Belarus and its people.

Early years and political career of Alexander Lukashenko

Alexander Lukashenko, often referred to as Europe's longest ruling dictator, has had a significant impact on Belarus and its people throughout his political career. To fully understand Lukashenko's rise to power and the subsequent consequences of his rule, it is important to delve into his early years and political beginnings.

Born on August 30, 1954, in the village of Kopys, in the Soviet Union, Lukashenko hailed from a humble background. He grew up in a working-class family and later pursued a career in agriculture, obtaining a degree in agricultural engineering from the Mogilev Agricultural Institute. This background would later shape his economic policies and focus on agricultural development in Belarus.

Lukashenko began his political career in the late 1980s during the perestroika period, a time of political and social change in the Soviet Union. He entered politics as a member of the Communist Party, and his rise to power was fueled by a populist appeal to the working class and promises of stability and prosperity.

In 1994, Lukashenko successfully campaigned for the presidency of Belarus and assumed office in July of that year. From the beginning, his rule was characterized by a consolidation of power and a disregard for democratic principles. Lukashenko quickly implemented policies that curtailed political dissent and suppressed opposition movements, leading to widespread human rights violations in the country.

Furthermore, Lukashenko's close ties with Russia have had a profound impact on Belarus' foreign policy and relations with neighboring countries. He has consistently sought to strengthen the alliance with

Russia, often at the expense of Belarus' relations with the European Union and other Western nations.

Lukashenko's control over the media and freedom of speech has been a defining feature of his regime. Independent media outlets have been systematically silenced, and journalists critical of the government have faced intimidation, harassment, and imprisonment. This control over information has allowed Lukashenko to maintain a tight grip on power and suppress any opposition voices.

Despite the challenges posed by Lukashenko's regime, there have been opposition movements in Belarus that have tirelessly fought against his rule. These movements, composed of civil society organizations, activists, and opposition politicians, have faced immense repression but have continued to push for democratic reforms and human rights.

Internationally, Lukashenko's dictatorship has been met with criticism and condemnation. The European Union and the United States have imposed sanctions on Belarus in response to human rights abuses and electoral fraud. However, Lukashenko has remained resilient and has managed to maintain his grip on power.

As Lukashenko's rule continues, the future of Belarus without him remains uncertain. His influence on Belarusian culture and arts, as well as the country's economic policies, will undoubtedly shape the path forward. Furthermore, his foreign policy decisions will continue to impact Belarus' relations with the EU and neighboring countries.

In conclusion, Alexander Lukashenko's early years and political career have had far-reaching consequences, both domestically and internationally. His consolidation of power, suppression of political dissent, human rights violations, and control over the media have defined his regime. The struggle of opposition movements and the international response to his dictatorship have shed light on the need for democratic reforms and respect for human rights in Belarus. As historians, it is crucial to analyze Lukashenko's legacy and the future of Belarus without him, while also examining the impact of his economic policies and foreign relations on the country and its people.

Consolidation of power and establishment of authoritarian rule

In the subchapter "Consolidation of power and establishment of authoritarian rule," we delve into the historical analysis of Alexander Lukashenko's regime, shedding light on the methods he employed to tighten his grip on power and establish an authoritarian rule in Belarus. This chapter aims to provide a comprehensive understanding of the key events and strategies that characterized Lukashenko's reign, primarily for historians and those interested in studying Europe's longest ruling dictator.

Throughout his tenure, Lukashenko utilized various tactics to consolidate his power. One of the most significant aspects was his manipulation of the political system, gradually altering the constitution to enhance his authority and weaken checks and balances. By centralizing power in the presidency, Lukashenko effectively marginalized other branches of government and reinforced his authoritarian rule.

Moreover, this chapter delves into Lukashenko's economic policies and their impact on Belarus. By pursuing a state-centric economic model, he aimed to consolidate control over key industries, leading to a highly centralized economy. While these policies initially brought stability and economic growth, they also resulted in widespread corruption, inefficiencies, and a lack of diversification, leaving Belarus heavily reliant on Russia.

Another crucial aspect covered in this subchapter is Lukashenko's suppression of political dissent. Throughout his rule, he systematically silenced opposition voices, employing tactics such as intimidation, harassment, and imprisonment. The human rights violations under his regime are extensively examined, shedding light on the suppression of freedom of speech, assembly, and association.

Furthermore, the subchapter explores Lukashenko's relationship with Russia and its implications for Belarus. His close ties with Moscow allowed him to maintain political and economic support, but it also subjected Belarus to Russian influence, compromising its sovereignty. The chapter also highlights Lukashenko's control over the media and freedom of speech in Belarus, which played a pivotal role in maintaining his authoritarian rule.

Additionally, the resistance of Belarusian opposition movements against Lukashenko's regime is examined, showcasing their struggle for democracy and human rights. The international response to Lukashenko's dictatorship is also explored, highlighting both diplomatic and economic measures taken by the international community to address his oppressive rule.

Lastly, this subchapter touches upon Alexander Lukashenko's influence on Belarusian culture and arts. It explores the ways in which his regime sought to shape cultural narratives and control artistic expression, ultimately impacting the nation's cultural identity.

In conclusion, this subchapter provides a comprehensive analysis of the consolidation of power and establishment of authoritarian rule under Alexander Lukashenko's regime. By examining the key aspects of his rule, including political manipulation, economic policies, suppression of dissent, relationship with Russia, control over the media, and impact on Belarusian culture, historians can gain valuable insights into Europe's longest ruling dictator and his lasting legacy on Belarus.

Chapter 2: Alexander Lukashenko's Economic Policies and Their Impact on Belarus

Overview of Lukashenko's economic ideology

Alexander Lukashenko, Europe's longest ruling dictator, has implemented a unique economic ideology during his time in power in Belarus. This subchapter aims to provide a comprehensive overview of Lukashenko's economic policies and their impact on the country.

Lukashenko's economic ideology can be best described as a blend of state socialism and authoritarian capitalism. His regime has maintained a strong grip on the economy, with the government controlling key industries and resources. This centralized approach has allowed Lukashenko to exert significant control over the country's economic development and ensure stability.

Under Lukashenko's rule, Belarus has pursued a policy of economic self-sufficiency, prioritizing domestic production and reducing reliance on imports. This has been achieved through protectionist measures, subsidies, and state intervention in the market. The government has also implemented strict currency controls and maintained a fixed exchange rate to stabilize the economy.

One of the key features of Lukashenko's economic policies has been the emphasis on maintaining social welfare programs. Despite the criticism of his political regime, Lukashenko has successfully implemented various social programs, including generous pensions, healthcare, and education. These policies have helped to alleviate poverty and improve living standards for many Belarusians.

However, Lukashenko's economic ideology has also been marred by inefficiencies, corruption, and a lack of economic diversification. The state-controlled economy has hindered innovation and entrepreneurship, leading to a stagnant private sector. The absence of a competitive market has resulted in limited consumer choices and a lack of investment in critical sectors.

Moreover, Lukashenko's economic policies have also contributed to a highly centralized power structure, with the state exerting control over the media and limiting freedom of speech. This has stifled political dissent and hindered the development of a vibrant civil society.

Looking ahead, Lukashenko's economic ideology and its impact on Belarus will continue to shape the country's future. As his regime faces growing international pressure and internal opposition, the question of economic reform and diversification becomes crucial for the country's stability and prosperity.

In conclusion, Lukashenko's economic ideology, characterized by a blend of state socialism and authoritarian capitalism, has had a significant impact on Belarus. While it has brought stability and social welfare programs, it has also hindered economic diversification and stifled political dissent. The future of Belarus without Lukashenko will depend on the ability to address these economic challenges and transition towards a more open and competitive economy.

State control and nationalization of industries

One of the key aspects of Alexander Lukashenko's economic policies in Belarus has been the state control and nationalization of industries. This subchapter explores the impact of these policies on the country's economy and society, providing insights into Lukashenko's governance style as Europe's longest ruling dictator.

Lukashenko's regime has exhibited a strong emphasis on state control over key industries, such as energy, agriculture, and manufacturing. This approach stems from his belief in the importance of maintaining a centralized economy to ensure stability and control. Under his leadership, the government has actively pursued the nationalization of major companies, often targeting those with significant economic influence.

The nationalization process has been characterized by the transfer of ownership and control from private hands to the state. This has led to the consolidation of power in Lukashenko's hands, as he gains more control over key sectors of the economy. The government's rationale for nationalization is often framed as a means to protect national interests and ensure economic self-sufficiency.

However, critics argue that the state control and nationalization of industries have resulted in a lack of competition, inefficiency, and corruption. The absence of a free market has hindered innovation and stifled economic growth. Furthermore, the lack of transparency in the decision-making process has raised concerns about accountability and the misuse of public funds.

In addition to economic implications, state control and nationalization have also had a profound impact on political dissent and human rights in Belarus. The concentration of power in the hands of the state has allowed Lukashenko to suppress political opposition and curtail freedom of speech. Independent media outlets have been targeted, resulting in a lack of diverse perspectives and critical voices.

The international response to Lukashenko's regime has been mixed. While some countries have criticized his authoritarian style of governance, others, such as Russia, have supported his policies, viewing him as a strategic ally. This has further complicated Belarus' relations with the European Union and neighboring countries, as Lukashenko's foreign policy aligns more closely with Russia's interests.

As historians analyze Lukashenko's economic policies, it is crucial to examine their impact on Belarusian society and the country's future without him. The nationalization of industries has shaped the country's economic landscape and governance model, leaving a lasting legacy that will continue to influence Belarus' trajectory. Understanding this aspect of Lukashenko's rule is essential for comprehending the broader dynamics of his regime and its implications for Belarusian society.

Agricultural policies and impact on the rural sector

One of the most significant aspects of Alexander Lukashenko's rule in Belarus is undoubtedly his agricultural policies and their impact on the rural sector. Understanding the implications of these policies is crucial in comprehending the broader context of Lukashenko's governance and its effects on Belarusian society.

Lukashenko's agricultural policies have been characterized by a strong emphasis on state control and collectivization. Since coming to power in 1994, he has pursued a strategy of consolidating the country's agricultural sector under state-controlled farms and cooperatives. This approach, often referred to as "agricultural socialism," has had profound consequences for the rural sector.

On one hand, these policies have ensured a degree of stability in the agriculture industry. State control has allowed for better planning and coordination, leading to increased productivity and food security. Moreover, Lukashenko's government has provided significant subsidies and support to farmers, ensuring their livelihoods and incentivizing agricultural production.

However, the centralized nature of Belarusian agriculture has also resulted in several challenges. The lack of private ownership and market-oriented reforms has hindered innovation and efficiency. Farmers have limited autonomy and face restrictions in decision-making, stifling their entrepreneurial spirit. Additionally, the state's control over the sector has led to issues of corruption and mismanagement, which have further undermined the potential growth of the rural economy.

Moreover, Lukashenko's agricultural policies have also had social consequences. The collectivization of land and agricultural resources has disrupted traditional rural communities and their way of life. Many small-scale farmers have been forced to give up their land and join state-run farms, eroding the fabric of rural society. This has led to a loss of cultural heritage and identity, as well as a decline in social cohesion within rural communities.

In conclusion, Lukashenko's agricultural policies have had a significant impact on the rural sector in Belarus. While they have provided stability and support to the industry, they have also hindered innovation and autonomy. Moreover, the collectivization process has disrupted traditional rural communities, leading to social and cultural consequences. Understanding these policies is crucial in comprehending the broader implications of Lukashenko's rule and its effects on Belarusian society.

Economic stagnation and reliance on Russia

In the realm of economic policy, Alexander Lukashenko's reign has been marked by a persistent state of stagnation in Belarus, coupled with an overwhelming dependence on Russia. This subchapter aims to delve into the intricacies of Lukashenko's economic policies, their impact on Belarus, and the country's reliance on its powerful neighbor.

Under Lukashenko's rule, Belarus has witnessed a lack of diversification in its economy, leading to a heavy reliance on traditional industries such as agriculture and manufacturing. This narrow focus has hindered the country's ability to adapt to global economic changes and compete on an international level. As a result, Belarus has struggled to attract foreign direct investment, limiting its economic growth potential.

Furthermore, Lukashenko's economic policies have often prioritized state control and protectionism over market liberalization and innovation. State-owned enterprises dominate key sectors of the economy, stifling private sector growth and entrepreneurship. The lack of competition and inefficiencies within these state-owned enterprises have contributed to the overall sluggishness of the Belarusian economy.

A significant factor in Belarus' economic stagnation is its heavy reliance on Russia. Lukashenko has consistently maintained close ties with the Kremlin, relying on subsidized oil and gas imports from Russia to sustain the country's energy needs. This dependence has made Belarus vulnerable to fluctuations in global energy prices and Russia's political agenda. With Russia's economic leverage, Lukashenko has had limited room to maneuver independently and pursue alternative economic partnerships.

The economic stagnation and reliance on Russia have had profound consequences for the people of Belarus. The lack of economic opportunities, rising inflation, and low wages have fueled public discontent and led to mass emigration. The brain drain has further damaged the country's economic prospects, as skilled professionals seek better opportunities abroad.

In conclusion, Lukashenko's economic policies, characterized by a lack of diversification, state control, and dependence on Russia, have contributed to Belarus' economic stagnation. The country's reliance on traditional industries and limited foreign investment has hampered its growth potential. As the future of Belarus unfolds, addressing these economic challenges and reducing dependence on Russia will be crucial for the country's prosperity and stability.

Chapter 3: Alexander Lukashenko's Suppression of Political Dissent in Belarus

Establishment of a repressive regime

In the subchapter "Establishment of a repressive regime," we delve into the origins and evolution of Alexander Lukashenko's dictatorial rule in Belarus. This chapter aims to provide historians with a comprehensive understanding of how Lukashenko transformed Belarus into Europe's longest-running dictatorship.

Alexander Lukashenko's ascent to power in 1994 marked a turning point in Belarusian history. Initially elected with promises of democratic reforms and economic prosperity, Lukashenko gradually consolidated power and established a repressive regime that has endured for over two decades.

Lukashenko's economic policies played a crucial role in the consolidation of his regime. By exerting control over key industries and implementing protectionist measures, Lukashenko stifled competition and maintained a firm grip on the country's economy. However, these policies had detrimental effects on Belarus' economic growth and independence, leading to dependence on Russia and a decline in living standards for the Belarusian people.

One of the most notorious aspects of Lukashenko's regime is his suppression of political dissent. Through a combination of legal restrictions, intimidation tactics, and the manipulation of elections, Lukashenko silenced opposition voices and undermined democratic institutions. This subchapter explores the various methods employed by Lukashenko to suppress political dissent and maintain his grip on power.

Human rights violations have been rampant under Lukashenko's rule, with reports of arbitrary arrests, torture, and mistreatment of prisoners. This subchapter delves into the extent of these violations, shedding light on the systematic abuse of human rights in Belarus.

Lukashenko's close relationship with Russia has also had significant implications for Belarus. This subchapter analyzes the dynamics of this relationship and its impact on Belarus' sovereignty and independence. It explores the influence Russia has exerted over Lukashenko's policies and the implications for Belarus' relations with the European Union and neighboring countries.

Another crucial element of Lukashenko's regime is his control over the media and freedom of speech. This subchapter delves into the mechanisms through which Lukashenko has suppressed independent media outlets, stifled dissenting voices, and manipulated public opinion.

Belarusian opposition movements have continually struggled against Lukashenko's rule. This subchapter explores the challenges faced by these movements, their strategies for mobilization, and the impact of their activism on the political landscape of Belarus.

The international response to Lukashenko's dictatorship has been varied, ranging from condemnation to diplomatic engagement. This subchapter analyzes the different approaches taken by the international community and their effectiveness in promoting democracy and human rights in Belarus.

Lastly, this subchapter examines Lukashenko's influence on Belarusian culture and the arts. It explores the ways in which Lukashenko's regime has shaped and restricted artistic expression, as well as the resilience of artists and cultural figures in the face of repression.

By examining the establishment of Lukashenko's repressive regime, historians gain valuable insights into the complexities of his rule and its multifaceted impact on Belarus and the international community. Understanding this historical context is crucial for comprehending Lukashenko's legacy and envisioning the future of Belarus without him.

Crackdown on opposition parties and politicians

In the realm of Alexander Lukashenko's authoritarian rule, one aspect that has been particularly pronounced is the relentless crackdown on opposition parties and politicians. This subchapter explores the systematic suppression of political dissent in Belarus under Lukashenko's regime, shedding light on the tactics employed, the consequences faced by opposition figures, and the implications for the country's political landscape.

From the very beginning of his rule in 1994, Lukashenko has employed various strategies to maintain an iron grip on power, including the manipulation of electoral processes and the marginalization of opposition parties. Through a combination of restrictive legislation, intimidation, and harassment, the regime has effectively suppressed any dissenting voices, leaving little room for a genuine multiparty system to flourish.

Opposition politicians in Belarus have faced numerous challenges, including arbitrary arrests, trumped-up charges, and even forced exile. Many have been subjected to physical violence, often at the hands of state security forces. Those brave enough to challenge Lukashenko's authority have been met with fierce resistance, with their political careers and personal lives often left in ruins.

The crackdown on opposition parties and politicians has had far-reaching consequences for the political landscape of Belarus. With no viable alternatives to Lukashenko's rule, the country has been left without a legitimate opposition capable of challenging his policies or holding him accountable. This lack of political competition has perpetuated a culture of fear and apathy, stifling the growth of a vibrant democratic system.

Furthermore, the suppression of political dissent has resulted in a severe curtailment of civil liberties and human rights in Belarus. Freedom of speech, assembly, and association have all been systematically undermined, leaving citizens in a state of constant surveillance and fear. The regime's control over the media has further contributed to the silencing of opposition voices, with independent journalists facing harassment and intimidation.

The international community has been swift to condemn Lukashenko's crackdown on opposition parties and politicians. Sanctions and diplomatic pressure have been applied to try and alleviate the suffering of those affected by the regime's repressive tactics. However, Lukashenko's relationship with Russia has provided a shield against more severe consequences, with the Kremlin offering support and protection.

In conclusion, the crackdown on opposition parties and politicians under Alexander Lukashenko's regime has had a profound impact on the political, social, and human rights landscape of Belarus. The complete suppression of dissent has left the country without a genuine opposition, perpetuating a one-party rule that hampers the development of a democratic system. The international response to Lukashenko's dictatorship has been mixed, with limited success in curbing his repressive tactics. As historians, it is crucial to document and analyze these events to shed light on the legacy of Europe's longest-ruling dictator and the future of Belarus without him.

Surveillance and control of civil society organizations

In the subchapter titled "Surveillance and Control of Civil Society Organizations" from the book "Alexander Lukashenko: A Historical Analysis of Europe's Longest Ruling Dictator," we delve into the systematic monitoring, manipulation, and suppression of civil society organizations under Lukashenko's regime in Belarus. This chapter provides a comprehensive examination of how Lukashenko has used surveillance and control tactics to stifle dissent and maintain his grip on power.

Throughout his reign, Lukashenko has implemented a range of measures to surveil and control civil society organizations. These organizations, which play a crucial role in advocating for human rights, democracy, and social justice, have faced immense scrutiny and interference from the government. Lukashenko's administration has employed extensive surveillance techniques, including wiretapping, infiltration, and monitoring of communication channels, to keep a close eye on civil society actors and their activities.

The aim of this surveillance is to intimidate and deter civil society organizations from engaging in activities that challenge Lukashenko's authority. By constantly monitoring their actions and communications, the regime seeks to suppress dissent, limit the scope of their work, and maintain a stranglehold on power. This surveillance apparatus has created an atmosphere of fear and self-censorship among civil society actors, as they are constantly aware of being watched and potentially punished for their actions.

Furthermore, Lukashenko's regime has imposed strict control mechanisms on civil society organizations, effectively limiting their independence and autonomy. The government has enacted restrictive legislation, imposed burdensome registration processes, and used bureaucratic hurdles to hinder the functioning of these organizations. Additionally, Lukashenko's regime has selectively targeted and harassed prominent activists and leaders, further undermining the effectiveness of civil society movements.

The consequences of surveillance and control of civil society organizations under Lukashenko's rule have been far-reaching. The suppression of dissent has led to a shrinking space for civic engagement, as individuals and organizations fear reprisals for challenging the status quo. This has resulted in a stifling of democratic processes, a lack of accountability, and a disregard for human rights.

The implications of this surveillance and control extend beyond the borders of Belarus. The international community has been alarmed by Lukashenko's tactics, and many have condemned his actions. However, the response from neighboring countries and the European Union has been mixed, with some opting for economic and diplomatic engagement, while others have imposed sanctions and sought to isolate Lukashenko's regime.

In conclusion, the subchapter "Surveillance and Control of Civil Society Organizations" sheds light on the alarming tactics employed by Alexander Lukashenko to stifle dissent and maintain his authoritarian rule. By examining the surveillance methods and control mechanisms used against civil society actors, historians gain a deeper understanding of the challenges faced by those striving for democracy, human rights, and social justice in Belarus. The analysis serves as a reminder of the importance of safeguarding civil society organizations and the need for international solidarity in the face of oppressive regimes.

Implications for political freedom and human rights

The subchapter titled "Implications for Political Freedom and Human Rights" in the book "Alexander Lukashenko: A Historical Analysis of Europe's Longest Ruling Dictator" delves into the significant consequences of Lukashenko's regime on the political freedom and human rights landscape in Belarus. This section seeks to provide a comprehensive understanding of the impact of Lukashenko's authoritarian rule on these crucial aspects of society.

Lukashenko's grip on power has had dire implications for political freedom in Belarus. Throughout his tenure, he has systematically suppressed political dissent and curtailed the activities of opposition movements. This subchapter explores the various tactics employed by Lukashenko to silence his critics, including arbitrary arrests, intimidation, and even violence. By analyzing specific cases, it sheds light on the extent to which political dissent has been suppressed under his regime.

Moreover, the subchapter examines the numerous human rights violations that have occurred under Lukashenko's rule. It delves into the infringement of civil liberties, such as freedom of speech, assembly, and association, providing examples of how these rights have been curtailed. Furthermore, it explores the mistreatment and imprisonment of individuals who have dared to challenge Lukashenko's authority, shedding light on the grave violations of human rights that have taken place under his regime.

Another crucial aspect discussed in this subchapter is Lukashenko's control over the media and freedom of speech in Belarus. It delves into his manipulation of the media landscape to ensure that only his narrative is disseminated, stifling any dissenting voices. By exploring specific cases of censorship and propaganda, it highlights the far-reaching consequences of this control on the formation of public opinion and political discourse within the country.

The implications of Lukashenko's regime on human rights and political freedom extend beyond Belarus' borders. This subchapter also delves into the international response to Lukashenko's dictatorship, exploring the actions taken by the international community, including sanctions and condemnation. It also examines the implications of Lukashenko's relationship with Russia on Belarus' political freedom and human rights, shedding light on the complex dynamics of this alliance.

In conclusion, the subchapter "Implications for Political Freedom and Human Rights" provides a comprehensive analysis of the impact of Lukashenko's authoritarian rule on these crucial aspects of society. By examining the suppression of political dissent, human rights violations, control over the media, and the international response, it offers historians a valuable insight into the implications of Lukashenko's regime on political freedom and human rights in Belarus.

Chapter 4: Human Rights Violations under Alexander Lukashenko's Regime

Systematic violations of civil and political rights

Alexander Lukashenko's regime in Belarus has been marked by a series of systematic violations of civil and political rights. This subchapter delves into the deeply concerning human rights situation under Lukashenko's rule, shedding light on the various ways in which his regime has stifled dissent, suppressed opposition movements, controlled the media, and curtailed freedom of speech.

From the outset of his presidency in 1994, Lukashenko consolidated power by eroding the checks and balances that are essential for a functioning democracy. He manipulated the constitution to extend his term limits and concentrated power in the executive branch, effectively diminishing the role of the parliament and judiciary. This consolidation of power has allowed his regime to perpetuate numerous human rights abuses.

One of the most egregious violations has been the systematic suppression of political dissent. Lukashenko's regime has relentlessly targeted opposition movements, imprisoning political opponents, and resorting to intimidation tactics to silence dissenting voices. The subjugation of opposition leaders and activists through arbitrary arrests, torture, and forced disappearances has become a hallmark of Lukashenko's rule.

Furthermore, Lukashenko has exerted strict control over the media and freedom of speech. Independent media outlets have been systematically shut down or heavily censored, leaving the state-controlled media as the primary source of information for the Belarusian population. This control over the media has allowed Lukashenko to manipulate public opinion and suppress any criticism of his regime.

The international response to Lukashenko's dictatorship has been mixed. While some countries have condemned his human rights abuses and implemented sanctions, others, particularly Russia, have been more supportive of his regime. Lukashenko's close ties with Russia have not only bolstered his grip on power but have also had implications for Belarus' relationship with the European Union and neighboring countries.

In conclusion, the systematic violations of civil and political rights under Alexander Lukashenko's regime have had a devastating impact on the people of Belarus. The suppression of political dissent, control over the media, and curtailment of freedom of speech have eroded the foundations of democracy and stifled any opposition to his rule. The international community must continue to pressure Lukashenko's regime to respect human rights and work towards a future for Belarus that embraces freedom, democracy, and respect for civil liberties.

Torture, arbitrary arrests, and disappearances

The subchapter titled "Torture, arbitrary arrests, and disappearances" delves into the dark underbelly of Alexander Lukashenko's regime, exploring the egregious human rights violations that have been rampant in Belarus for over two decades. This chapter aims to shed light on the systematic suppression of dissent, the use of torture, and the arbitrary arrests and disappearances that have plagued the country under Lukashenko's rule.

Throughout Lukashenko's tenure, Belarus has witnessed a disturbing pattern of torture and mistreatment of individuals who dare to challenge the regime. Dissidents, human rights activists, journalists, and political opponents have all been subjected to brutal forms of torture, such as beatings, electric shocks, and psychological abuse. These methods are employed to suppress any form of opposition and to instill fear within the population.

Arbitrary arrests have become a hallmark of Lukashenko's regime. Individuals are often detained without proper legal procedures, with no access to legal representation, and for extended periods of time. The regime frequently uses trumped-up charges to justify these arrests, ensuring that any perceived threats to the regime are swiftly silenced.

Perhaps most chilling are the disappearances that have occurred under Lukashenko's rule. Activists and opposition figures have been known to vanish without a trace, leaving their families and loved ones in a state of perpetual anguish. These disappearances serve as a stark reminder of the regime's power and its willingness to go to any lengths to maintain control.

The impact of these human rights violations on the people of Belarus cannot be overstated. The culture of fear and repression has stifled freedom of expression, creating an environment where individuals are afraid to speak out against the regime. Dissent is met with severe consequences, leading to a silencing of voices and a perpetuation of Lukashenko's autocratic rule.

As historians, it is crucial to document and analyze these atrocities, ensuring that they are not forgotten or brushed aside. By shedding light on the torture, arbitrary arrests, and disappearances that have occurred under Lukashenko's rule, we can contribute to a comprehensive understanding of his regime and the long-lasting impact it has had on Belarusian society.

This subchapter serves as a stark reminder of the violations committed under Lukashenko's rule and allows us to question the future of Belarus without him. It prompts further exploration into the international response to his dictatorship, the struggle of Belarusian opposition movements, and the implications of his foreign policy on Belarus' relations with the EU and neighboring countries. By examining and understanding these facets, historians can help shape a better future for Belarus, one that upholds human rights, democracy, and freedom.

Restriction of freedom of expression and assembly

In the realm of authoritarian regimes, few leaders have been as notorious as Alexander Lukashenko, Europe's longest-ruling dictator. Throughout his decades-long reign, Lukashenko has consistently employed various tactics to restrict freedom of expression and assembly in Belarus. This subchapter delves into the systematic suppression of these fundamental rights under his regime, shedding light on the impact it has had on the country and its people.

Lukashenko's control over the media and freedom of speech has been a cornerstone of his authoritarian rule. Independent journalism and critical voices have been systematically silenced, as the regime has tightened its grip on the media landscape. Government-controlled media outlets dominate the airwaves, disseminating propaganda and promoting Lukashenko's narrative, effectively stifling any dissenting views. Journalists who dare to challenge this narrative face severe consequences, including harassment, imprisonment, or forced exile.

Furthermore, Lukashenko's regime has engaged in a relentless crackdown on peaceful protests and assemblies. The right to gather and voice one's opinions freely has been consistently undermined, with the authorities resorting to violent tactics to suppress any form of dissent. Peaceful demonstrators have been met with brutal force, arbitrary arrests, and politically motivated prosecutions. Civil society organizations, opposition movements, and activists advocating for change have faced immense pressure, making it increasingly difficult for them to operate.

The human rights violations under Lukashenko's regime are alarming and well-documented. From arbitrary detentions to torture and disappearances, the regime has shown little regard for the basic rights and dignity of its citizens. The international community has repeatedly condemned these violations, calling for an end to the repression and the release of political prisoners.

Despite these restrictions, Belarusian opposition movements persist and struggle against Lukashenko's rule. Brave individuals have emerged as symbols of resistance, challenging the regime's suppression and advocating for democratic change. Their resilience and determination provide hope for a brighter future for Belarus, free from the clutches of Lukashenko's dictatorship.

As historians, it is crucial to document and analyze the impact of Lukashenko's restriction on freedom of expression and assembly. By understanding the mechanisms of repression employed by his regime, we can shed light on the resilience of the Belarusian people and the potential for change. Only through this comprehensive understanding can we envision a future where Belarus can emerge from the shadow of Lukashenko's legacy and embrace a democratic and free society.

International condemnation and human rights reports

One aspect that has garnered significant attention in understanding the rule of Alexander Lukashenko is the international condemnation and human rights reports that have shed light on the state of affairs in Belarus. Lukashenko's regime has been widely criticized by various international organizations and governments for its flagrant disregard for human rights and democratic principles.

Human rights violations under Lukashenko's regime have been well-documented. Reports from organizations such as Human Rights Watch and Amnesty International have highlighted the widespread use of torture, arbitrary arrests, and unfair trials against political dissidents, journalists, and activists. Freedom of speech and assembly are severely curtailed, with opposition voices being silenced and independent media outlets facing constant harassment and censorship.

The international response to Lukashenko's dictatorship has been mixed. While some governments and organizations have taken a strong stance against his regime, imposing sanctions and condemning his actions, others have maintained diplomatic relations, often driven by their own geopolitical interests. The European Union, for instance, has imposed targeted sanctions on Belarusian officials and has repeatedly called for the release of political prisoners. However, Lukashenko's close ties with Russia, which has been accused of supporting his authoritarian rule, have complicated international efforts to exert pressure on his regime.

The human rights situation in Belarus has also been a topic of discussion in various international forums such as the United Nations and the Organization for Security and Cooperation in Europe (OSCE). These platforms provide an opportunity for governments and civil society organizations to raise concerns and push for accountability. However, the effectiveness of these mechanisms in bringing about meaningful change in Belarus remains a subject of debate.

Understanding the international condemnation and human rights reports is crucial not only for historians studying Lukashenko's reign but also for those interested in the broader context of human rights abuses and authoritarian regimes. It raises important questions about the role of the international community in addressing such violations and the effectiveness of various mechanisms in holding dictators accountable.

As historians delve into the historical analysis of Europe's longest ruling dictator, it is imperative to examine the international response to Lukashenko's regime and the human rights reports that have played a significant role in shaping global perceptions of his rule. This subchapter provides a comprehensive overview of the international condemnation and human rights reports, shedding light on the atrocities committed under Lukashenko's rule and the efforts made by the international community to address them.

Chapter 5: Alexander Lukashenko's Relationship with Russia and Its Implications for Belarus

Historical context of Belarus-Russia relations

Belarus-Russia relations have a long and complex history that dates back several centuries. Understanding the historical context of this relationship is crucial in comprehending the dynamics of Alexander Lukashenko's regime and its implications for Belarus. This subchapter will delve into the intricacies of this historical context, shedding light on the enduring ties between these two nations.

The history of Belarus-Russia relations can be traced back to the medieval era when Belarus was part of the Grand Duchy of Lithuania. The union between Lithuania and Poland in the 16th century marked the beginning of a period of Polish influence in the region, which lasted for several centuries. However, the Russian Empire's expansionism in the 18th century led to Belarus becoming a part of the Russian Empire.

The Soviet era played a significant role in shaping the Belarus-Russia relations as we know them today. Both Belarus and Russia were part of the Soviet Union, which lasted from 1922 to 1991. During this period, Belarus experienced Russification policies, which aimed to suppress Belarusian national identity and promote Russian culture and language. These policies had a lasting impact on the Belarusian people and their relationship with Russia.

Following the collapse of the Soviet Union, Belarus gained independence in 1991. However, its ties with Russia remained strong due to historical, cultural, and economic factors. Alexander Lukashenko's rise to power in 1994 further solidified these ties. Lukashenko adopted a pro-Russian stance, emphasizing the importance of the "Slavic brotherhood" and aligning Belarus with Russia's political and economic interests.

Lukashenko's close relationship with Russia has had significant implications for Belarus. Economically, Belarus has heavily relied on Russian subsidies, energy imports, and trade partnerships. However, this dependency has also put Belarus at the mercy of Russian influence and control. Lukashenko's economic policies, while initially successful in stabilizing the country's economy, have resulted in stagnation and limited economic diversification.

Furthermore, Lukashenko's regime has been marked by the suppression of political dissent and human rights violations. This has strained Belarus's relationship with the European Union and neighboring countries. The international response to Lukashenko's dictatorship has been one of condemnation and calls for democratic reforms.

In conclusion, the historical context of Belarus-Russia relations provides valuable insights into the dynamics of Alexander Lukashenko's regime and its implications for Belarus. Understanding the enduring ties between these nations helps shed light on Lukashenko's pro-Russian stance, economic policies, human rights violations, and the international response to his regime. It also highlights the challenges and opportunities that lie ahead for Belarus in a post-Lukashenko era, as it seeks to redefine its relationship with Russia and the European Union.

Lukashenko's balancing act between Russia and the West

In the complex geopolitical landscape of Belarus, Alexander Lukashenko has skillfully managed to navigate between two powerful forces: Russia and the West. Throughout his tenure as Europe's longest-ruling dictator, Lukashenko has maintained a delicate balance, carefully treading the line between these two competing spheres of influence.

Lukashenko's approach to foreign policy has always been pragmatic, driven by his desire to maintain Belarus' independence and sovereignty. On one hand, he has cultivated a close relationship with Russia, recognizing the economic and political benefits that come with aligning with its powerful neighbor. Belarus remains heavily dependent on Russian energy exports and trade, with Russia being its largest trading partner. The close ties extend beyond economic cooperation, as Lukashenko has also entered into military alliances with Russia, ensuring Belarus' security in a volatile region.

However, Lukashenko's approach to the West has been equally strategic. He has sought to maintain a certain level of engagement with European countries, particularly the European Union (EU), as a means to counterbalance Russia's influence. Belarus has pursued a policy of "multi-vector diplomacy," actively engaging with both Russia and the West, while carefully avoiding taking sides. This has allowed Lukashenko to leverage his position, extracting economic concessions from both sides, as they vie for influence in the region.

Although Lukashenko has made overtures to the West, his regime's suppression of political dissent and human rights violations have strained relations with European countries. The EU and the United States have imposed sanctions on Belarus, criticizing Lukashenko's authoritarian rule and lack of political freedoms. This has limited Lukashenko's ability to fully integrate with the EU and has led to a deterioration of relations with neighboring countries such as Poland and Lithuania.

Lukashenko's balancing act has also extended to the media and freedom of speech in Belarus. His regime has tightly controlled the media landscape, ensuring that dissenting voices are silenced and critical reporting is suppressed. Independent journalists and opposition figures have faced harassment, imprisonment, and even forced exile. This oppressive environment has limited the spread of information and stifled public discourse, further consolidating Lukashenko's grip on power.

As historians, it is crucial to analyze Lukashenko's foreign policy and its implications for Belarus. While his balancing act between Russia and the West has allowed him to maintain control and preserve Belarus' independence, it has come at the cost of political freedoms and human rights. Lukashenko's legacy is one of authoritarian rule, characterized by a tight grip on power and limited space for opposition movements to flourish.

The future of Belarus without Lukashenko remains uncertain. As his influence wanes, there are hopes for a more democratic and open society. However, the legacy of his regime will undoubtedly shape the country's transition and its relations with Russia, the West, and its neighboring countries.

In conclusion, Lukashenko's balancing act between Russia and the West has defined his foreign policy and shaped Belarus' position in the global arena. While his strategic maneuvering has allowed him to maintain control and preserve Belarus' independence, it has come at the cost of political freedoms, human rights, and strained international relations. As historians, it is essential to critically analyze and understand the implications of Lukashenko's foreign policy on Belarus and its future.

Economic and political dependence on Russia

The economic and political dependence on Russia has been a defining characteristic of Alexander Lukashenko's regime in Belarus. Throughout his reign as Europe's longest ruling dictator, Lukashenko's economic policies and his close ties with Russia have had a profound impact on the country's development, politics, and international relations.

Lukashenko's economic policies have been centered around maintaining a strong relationship with Russia, which has resulted in Belarus becoming heavily reliant on its neighbor for trade and financial support. The close economic ties between the two countries have been characterized by subsidized energy prices, preferential trade agreements, and financial aid from Russia, which have helped Lukashenko maintain his grip on power by ensuring stability and economic growth.

However, this dependence on Russia has come at a cost. The Belarusian economy has become highly vulnerable to fluctuations in the Russian economy, particularly in the energy sector. Any disruption in energy supplies or changes in energy prices can have a significant impact on Belarus' economic stability and growth. This vulnerability has made Belarus highly susceptible to Russian influence, making it difficult for the country to pursue independent economic policies or diversify its trade relations.

Moreover, the political dependence on Russia has also affected Belarus' domestic politics and human rights situation. Lukashenko's regime has used its close ties with Russia to suppress political dissent and maintain control over the media and freedom of speech. The government has consistently targeted opposition movements, human rights activists, and independent media outlets, using tactics such as arbitrary arrests, intimidation, and censorship. This repression has resulted in numerous human rights violations under Lukashenko's rule, leading to international condemnation and sanctions against Belarus.

Looking at the international response, Lukashenko's dictatorship has faced significant criticism from the international community. The European Union and neighboring countries have been vocal in their condemnation of human rights abuses and political repression in Belarus. This has resulted in sanctions and diplomatic pressure being placed on Lukashenko's regime, further isolating the country and limiting its opportunities for international cooperation and development.

As Lukashenko's reign continues, the question of Belarus' future without him becomes increasingly important. The legacy of Lukashenko's rule and his impact on Belarusian culture, arts, and foreign policy will shape the country's future, as well as its relations with the European Union and neighboring countries. However, it remains to be seen whether Belarus can break free from its economic and political dependence on Russia and pursue a path of independence, democracy, and respect for human rights.

Impact on Belarus' sovereignty and national identity

Belarus, under the long-standing rule of Alexander Lukashenko, has experienced significant implications on its sovereignty and national identity. This subchapter aims to delve into the multifaceted effects of Lukashenko's regime on these crucial aspects of the nation's existence.

Lukashenko's iron-fisted rule has undoubtedly eroded Belarus' sovereignty over the years. His consolidation of power through authoritarian measures has stifled democratic institutions, leaving Belarusians with limited avenues to exercise their rights and participate in decision-making processes. The suppression of political dissent and the crackdown on opposition movements have further curtailed the country's democratic potential, eroding the people's ability to express their political will freely.

Moreover, Lukashenko's control over the media and restriction of freedom of speech have played a pivotal role in shaping the national narrative. The state-controlled media has amplified the regime's propaganda, disseminating a biased portrayal of events and suppressing alternative viewpoints. This manipulation of information has had a profound impact on the formation of Belarusian national identity, as citizens are subjected to a narrow and distorted understanding of their own history and culture.

The regime's human rights violations have also left an indelible mark on Belarusian society. Peaceful protests have been met with violence, dissenters have been silenced through intimidation and imprisonment, and torture has been employed as a means of control. These grave violations have not only infringed upon individual liberties but have also challenged the nation's collective identity, raising questions about the values and principles Belarus seeks to uphold.

Furthermore, Lukashenko's close relationship with Russia has had implications for Belarus' sovereignty. While the alliance has provided economic benefits and security guarantees, it has also made Belarus susceptible to Moscow's influence. The increasing integration with Russia has raised concerns about the erosion of Belarus' independence and its ability to forge its own path on the international stage.

In conclusion, Alexander Lukashenko's long rule has had a profound impact on Belarus' sovereignty and national identity. The erosion of democratic institutions, suppression of dissent, human rights violations, and close ties with Russia have collectively shaped the nation's trajectory. Understanding these dynamics is crucial for historians seeking to comprehend the complexities of Lukashenko's regime and its lasting effects on Belarusian society.

Chapter 6: Alexander Lukashenko's Control over the Media and Freedom of Speech in Belarus

State control of media outlets

State control of media outlets is a crucial aspect of understanding Alexander Lukashenko's regime and its impact on Belarus. This subchapter delves into the mechanisms employed by Lukashenko to manipulate and suppress the media, ultimately stifling freedom of speech and information.

Lukashenko's control over the media is unparalleled, with a vast array of state-owned outlets serving as propaganda tools. These outlets, including television stations, newspapers, and radio stations, are strictly regulated by the government, ensuring that only pro-regime narratives are disseminated. Journalists who dare to challenge the official line are subject to harassment, intimidation, and even imprisonment.

By monopolizing the media, Lukashenko effectively silences opposition voices and maintains a tight grip on power. Independent media outlets are systematically marginalized and face constant pressure from the state. This has resulted in self-censorship and a climate of fear among journalists, severely limiting the diversity of viewpoints and impeding the free flow of information.

The consequences of state control over the media are far-reaching. Belarusian citizens are deprived of objective reporting, critical analysis, and alternative perspectives, hindering their ability to make informed decisions. The lack of transparency and accountability in governance allows Lukashenko to manipulate public opinion, perpetuating his authoritarian rule.

Furthermore, the suppression of media outlets and freedom of speech extends beyond national borders. Lukashenko's regime has targeted Belarusian dissidents and independent journalists abroad, employing tactics such as cyberattacks, physical violence, and even assassination attempts. This not only violates international norms but also contributes to a climate of fear among exiled Belarusians and the diaspora.

The international community has widely condemned Lukashenko's control over the media and its impact on human rights and democracy in Belarus. Sanctions, diplomatic pressure, and support for independent media initiatives have been deployed to counter these abuses. However, Lukashenko's alliance with Russia has allowed him to withstand international criticism, as Moscow has provided political and economic support, further complicating efforts to bring about change.

Understanding the extent of state control over media outlets is crucial to grasp the full scope of Lukashenko's authoritarian rule. Breaking this control will be essential for Belarus to transition towards a more democratic and open society, where freedom of speech and independent journalism can flourish. Only then can Belarusians enjoy true access to information and exercise their democratic rights without fear of reprisal.

Censorship and propaganda machinery

In the realm of authoritarian rule, the control over information and narrative becomes a crucial tool for maintaining power. This subchapter explores the mechanisms of censorship and propaganda machinery employed by Alexander Lukashenko, Europe's longest ruling dictator, in his quest to maintain an iron grip on Belarus.

Lukashenko's regime has implemented a multifaceted approach to control the media and manipulate public opinion. The state-owned media serves as the main mouthpiece, disseminating government-sanctioned narratives while suppressing dissenting voices.

Journalists critical of the regime are subjected to harassment, intimidation, and even imprisonment. This has resulted in a climate of fear, where self-censorship has become rampant, stifling any potential opposition.

The propaganda machinery operates through a variety of channels, including state-controlled television, radio, and newspapers. These outlets consistently promote Lukashenko's image as a strong and decisive leader, while demonizing opposition figures and dissenting voices. The regime utilizes strategic messaging to cultivate a sense of nationalism and loyalty towards Lukashenko, often portraying him as the only force capable of protecting Belarus from external threats.

Furthermore, the internet, once a potential platform for free expression, has also fallen victim to Lukashenko's censorship apparatus. The regime has imposed strict regulations and surveillance measures, blocking access to critical websites and social media platforms. Independent news outlets and opposition voices are routinely targeted, further limiting the flow of information and fostering an atmosphere of isolation.

The impact of this censorship and propaganda machinery on Belarusian society has been profound. It has not only suppressed political dissent but also eroded the public's trust in institutions and the media. The lack of access to unbiased information has hindered the development of an informed citizenry, inhibiting the growth of a democratic culture.

Understanding the methods employed by Lukashenko's regime is crucial for historians seeking to comprehend the dynamics of his long-lasting rule. By examining the censorship and propaganda machinery, we can gain insights into the manipulation tactics used to consolidate power and control public opinion. This subchapter delves into the intricate web of censorship, propaganda, and information control that has defined Lukashenko's regime, shedding light on the challenges faced by those striving for freedom of speech and expression in Belarus.

Persecution of independent journalists and media organizations

The persecution of independent journalists and media organizations under the regime of Alexander Lukashenko is a deeply troubling aspect of his rule. Throughout his tenure as Europe's longest ruling dictator, Lukashenko has consistently employed various tactics to suppress freedom of the press and control the narrative in Belarus.

Under Lukashenko's regime, independent journalists have faced intimidation, harassment, and imprisonment for their critical reporting. Media organizations that dare to challenge the government's narrative are subjected to censorship, forced closures, and arbitrary legal action. This systematic persecution has created a climate of fear, where journalists self-censor to avoid reprisals, compromising the integrity of the country's media landscape.

Lukashenko's control over the media extends beyond direct repression. He has consolidated state-owned media outlets, ensuring they serve as propaganda machines for his regime. Through state-controlled television, radio, and newspapers, Lukashenko tightly controls the flow of information, disseminating his narrative and suppressing dissenting voices.

The impact of this media control on Belarusian society is far-reaching. Citizens are denied access to unbiased reporting, diverse opinions, and alternative perspectives. As a result, public discourse is stifled, and critical thinking is undermined. The lack of media pluralism reinforces Lukashenko's grip on power, as he effectively monopolizes the narrative and manipulates public opinion.

This persecution of independent journalists and media organizations is not only a violation of freedom of speech but also a breach of human rights. It reflects a broader pattern of repression and authoritarianism under Lukashenko's rule. The international community has repeatedly condemned these violations, calling for the protection of journalists and media freedom in Belarus.

However, Lukashenko's regime has shown little regard for international criticism or pressure. His relationship with Russia has further enabled his suppression of independent media, as the Kremlin has supported his regime and provided a platform for his propaganda.

The struggle against Lukashenko's control over the media is an integral part of the Belarusian opposition movements' fight for democracy and human rights. Independent journalists and media organizations continue to face immense challenges, but their determination to expose the truth and hold the government accountable remains unwavering.

As historians, it is crucial to document and analyze the persecution of independent journalists and media organizations under Lukashenko's regime. By shedding light on these violations, we contribute to a comprehensive understanding of his rule and the impact it has had on Belarusian society. Only through this understanding can we envision a future where freedom of the press is safeguarded, and the voices of independent journalists are allowed to flourish.

Silencing dissent and the absence of freedom of speech

In the realm of authoritarian regimes, few leaders have mastered the art of silencing dissent and suppressing freedom of speech as effectively as Alexander Lukashenko, Europe's longest ruling dictator. This subchapter aims to shed light on the egregious violations of human rights under his regime, the control he exercises over the media, and the struggle faced by Belarusian opposition movements.

Lukashenko's iron grip on power has resulted in an environment where political dissent is met with harsh repercussions. Opposition leaders, journalists, and activists who dare to challenge his authority are subjected to intimidation, imprisonment, and even disappearances. The

Belarusian people live in constant fear, knowing that expressing their opinions may lead to dire consequences for themselves and their families.

One of the most alarming aspects of Lukashenko's rule is his control over the media and the restriction of freedom of speech. Independent news outlets are heavily censored, and journalists who dare to report on government corruption or criticize Lukashenko's policies are swiftly silenced. State-controlled media outlets serve as mouthpieces for the regime, disseminating propaganda and ensuring that only a skewed version of reality reaches the Belarusian public.

Despite the oppressive environment, Belarusian opposition movements persist in their struggle against Lukashenko's rule. Activists, civil society organizations, and political parties work tirelessly to promote democracy, human rights, and freedom of speech. However, their efforts are often met with violence, arbitrary arrests, and the dismantling of their organizations by the government.

The international response to Lukashenko's dictatorship has been mixed. While some countries and organizations have condemned his human rights abuses and imposed sanctions, others have maintained diplomatic relations, prioritizing political and economic interests over the well-being of the Belarusian people. The European Union, in particular, has taken a strong stance against Lukashenko, imposing sanctions and supporting the opposition movements.

Lukashenko's legacy and the future of Belarus without him are subjects of great interest and speculation. The impact of his economic policies, his relationship with Russia, and his foreign policy decisions have shaped Belarus' trajectory for the past two and a half decades. As his rule enters its twilight years, it is crucial for historians to analyze the consequences of his regime and envision a future for Belarus that upholds democratic values and respects human rights.

In conclusion, Alexander Lukashenko's suppression of political dissent and the absence of freedom of speech in Belarus have had far-reaching consequences for the country and its people. The violations of human rights, control over the media, and relentless oppression faced by opposition movements paint a bleak picture of Lukashenko's regime. As historians, it is our duty to document and analyze the impact of his rule, while also advocating for a future where Belarus can thrive as a free and democratic nation.

Chapter 7: Belarusian Opposition Movements and Their Struggle against Lukashenko's Rule

Emergence of opposition parties and movements

Throughout the reign of Alexander Lukashenko, the emergence of opposition parties and movements has been a significant aspect of Belarusian political history. As historians, it is crucial to analyze the development of these groups and understand their impact on the country's political landscape.

Lukashenko's iron grip on power, sustained by his authoritarian rule, has given rise to numerous opposition parties and movements. These organizations have sought to challenge his regime, advocating for democratic reforms, human rights, and freedom of speech in Belarus.

The formation of these opposition groups can be traced back to the early years of Lukashenko's rule. Dissatisfied with his autocratic style and oppressive policies, individuals from various backgrounds began to unite under a common goal of bringing about change. These groups represented a diverse range of ideologies, from liberal and social democratic to nationalist and pro-European.

Despite facing relentless repression and persecution from Lukashenko's regime, opposition parties and movements have consistently displayed resilience and determination. They have organized protests, demonstrations, and grassroots campaigns to raise awareness about human rights violations, political dissent, and the suppression of freedom of speech in Belarus.

The international community has closely observed the struggles of these opposition groups and lent support whenever possible. Despite

Lukashenko's efforts to isolate Belarus from the global stage, the voices of the opposition have managed to reach international platforms, shedding light on the dire situation faced by the Belarusian people under his rule.

The emergence of opposition parties and movements has not only served as a form of resistance but has also laid the groundwork for a potential democratic transition in the future. These groups have fostered a sense of unity among the Belarusian people, inspiring hope for a future where democratic values, human rights, and freedom of expression prevail.

As historians, it is important to document and analyze the emergence of these opposition parties and movements, as they represent a crucial chapter in the history of Alexander Lukashenko's dictatorship. By understanding their struggles, achievements, and setbacks, we can gain insights into the complex dynamics of Belarusian politics and the aspirations of its people.

In conclusion, the emergence of opposition parties and movements in Belarus has been a significant development during Alexander Lukashenko's long-lasting dictatorship. These groups have fought against his oppressive regime, advocating for democratic reforms and human rights. Their resilience and determination have inspired hope for a future where Belarus can break free from autocracy and embrace democratic values. As historians, it is our duty to study and analyze the impact of these opposition movements, as they represent an essential part of Belarusian history.

Challenges faced by the opposition in mobilizing support

Chapter 4: Challenges faced by the opposition in mobilizing support

Subchapter: Challenges faced by the opposition in mobilizing support

Throughout the history of Alexander Lukashenko's reign, the opposition in Belarus has faced numerous challenges in mobilizing support against the longest ruling dictator in Europe. These challenges have hindered their efforts to bring about change and establish a democratic system in the country.

One of the primary challenges faced by the opposition is the suppression of political dissent by Lukashenko's regime. The government has systematically targeted and persecuted opposition leaders, activists, and their supporters. Many have been imprisoned, harassed, or silenced, making it difficult for the opposition to mobilize and organize effectively.

Additionally, human rights violations under Lukashenko's regime have created a climate of fear and intimidation. This has further discouraged citizens from openly expressing their support for the opposition. Arbitrary arrests, torture, and disappearances have become common tactics used by the government to maintain control and discourage dissent.

Moreover, Lukashenko's control over the media and freedom of speech has made it challenging for the opposition to reach a wider audience. State-controlled media outlets have propagated pro-government narratives, while independent journalists and media organizations have faced restrictions and censorship. This lack of access to unbiased information has limited the opposition's ability to mobilize public support and raise awareness about their cause.

The opposition has also faced difficulties in gaining international support and recognition. While Lukashenko's regime has been widely criticized by the international community, concrete actions and sanctions have been limited. This has left the opposition feeling isolated and undermined their efforts to garner external assistance in their struggle against the dictatorship.

Furthermore, the opposition's fragmented nature and internal divisions have posed significant challenges. Infighting and a lack of unified strategy have weakened their ability to present a strong and cohesive alternative to Lukashenko's rule. This has hindered their ability to mobilize broad-based support and effectively challenge the regime.

In conclusion, the opposition in Belarus has faced numerous challenges in mobilizing support against Alexander Lukashenko's regime. The suppression of political dissent, human rights violations, control over the media, limited international support, and internal divisions have all contributed to the difficulties faced by the opposition. Despite these challenges, the opposition continues to persevere in their struggle for democracy and freedom in Belarus, hoping for a future where the country can thrive without the influence of Europe's longest ruling dictator.

Repression and persecution of opposition leaders

In the turbulent history of Alexander Lukashenko's rule, one of the most concerning aspects has been the relentless repression and persecution of opposition leaders in Belarus. Under his iron-fisted regime, political dissent is not tolerated, and anyone who dares to challenge his authority is swiftly silenced.

Lukashenko's grip on power has been maintained through a combination of intimidation tactics, manipulation of the legal system, and the suppression of political opposition. Opposition leaders are often subjected to harassment, arbitrary arrests, and even physical violence. Many have been unjustly imprisoned on trumped-up charges or forced into exile to avoid persecution.

The systematic targeting of opposition leaders has had a chilling effect on political discourse in Belarus. The fear of reprisals has created a climate of self-censorship, where individuals are reluctant to voice their opinions or engage in any form of political activism. This has stifled the development of a robust democratic culture and perpetuated Lukashenko's authoritarian rule.

The human rights violations under Lukashenko's regime extend far beyond the persecution of opposition leaders. Freedom of expression, assembly, and association are severely curtailed, with little room for dissenting voices. Independent media outlets have been shut down, journalists harassed, and critical voices silenced. The regime's control over the media has ensured a constant stream of propaganda, with little room for alternative viewpoints.

The international response to Lukashenko's repression has been mixed. While some countries and international organizations have condemned his actions and imposed sanctions, others have been reluctant to take a strong stance. This has emboldened Lukashenko and allowed him to continue his crackdown on political dissent with impunity.

It is crucial for historians to document the repression and persecution of opposition leaders under Lukashenko's rule. By shedding light on these abuses, we can ensure that the voices of those who have been silenced are not forgotten. Furthermore, understanding the tactics used by Lukashenko to maintain his grip on power can help inform future strategies to promote democracy and human rights in Belarus.

As historians, we must continue to study and analyze the repression and persecution of opposition leaders under Lukashenko's regime. By doing so, we can contribute to a comprehensive understanding of Europe's longest ruling dictator and his impact on Belarus. Only by confronting the dark chapters of history can we hope to build a future where human rights and democracy prevail in Belarus.

Prospects for democratic change in Belarus

The prospects for democratic change in Belarus have long been a topic of discussion and analysis among historians and scholars. In the book "Alexander Lukashenko: A Historical Analysis of Europe's Longest Ruling Dictator," this subchapter aims to shed light on the possibilities and challenges that lie ahead for Belarus in terms of democratic transformation.

Alexander Lukashenko's iron grip on power, as Europe's longest ruling dictator, has undoubtedly shaped the political landscape of Belarus. However, there are growing indications that the country is at a turning point, with opportunities for democratic change emerging.

One of the key factors influencing the prospects for democratic change in Belarus is the economic policies implemented by Lukashenko. Despite the initial stability and economic growth achieved, these policies have led to a stagnant economy and widespread corruption. This has created dissatisfaction among the population, fueling demands for change.

Lukashenko's suppression of political dissent has been one of the defining characteristics of his regime. However, the emergence of opposition movements and the resilience of civil society in Belarus cannot be overlooked. These movements, though often repressed, have shown a remarkable ability to mobilize and challenge Lukashenko's rule. Their struggle for political freedom and human rights is an important factor in shaping the prospects for democratic change.

The international response to Lukashenko's dictatorship has also played a role in influencing the prospects for democratic change. The European Union and neighboring countries have increasingly condemned his authoritarian rule and imposed sanctions. This has put pressure on Lukashenko and created opportunities for democratic forces to gain leverage.

Furthermore, Lukashenko's relationship with Russia and its implications for Belarus cannot be disregarded. While Russia has supported Lukashenko in the past, there are indications of a strained relationship. This could potentially create openings for democratic change, as Belarus seeks to redefine its relationship with both Russia and the European Union.

Looking ahead, the future of Belarus without Lukashenko raises questions about the country's political landscape, culture, and foreign policies. The legacy left by Lukashenko and his impact on Belarusian society will undoubtedly shape the path towards democracy.

In conclusion, while the prospects for democratic change in Belarus are not without challenges, there are clear indications that change is possible. The economic struggles, human rights violations, and growing opposition movements all contribute to a shifting political landscape. The international response and Lukashenko's relationship with Russia further add to the complexity of the situation. As historians, it is crucial to analyze these factors and examine the potential for democratic transformation in Belarus.

Chapter 8: The International Response to Alexander Lukashenko's Dictatorship

European Union sanctions and diplomatic pressure

European Union sanctions and diplomatic pressure have played a significant role in shaping the dynamics of Alexander Lukashenko's long-lasting dictatorship in Belarus. This subchapter delves into the impact of these measures and their implications for both Belarus and the European Union.

Lukashenko's authoritarian rule and his continuous suppression of political dissent have been met with condemnation from the international community, particularly the European Union. In response to Lukashenko's blatant disregard for human rights and democratic principles, the EU has imposed a series of sanctions on Belarus. These measures include travel bans and asset freezes on individuals and entities associated with the regime, as well as restrictions on financial transactions with Belarusian state-owned enterprises.

The primary objective of these sanctions is to exert diplomatic pressure on Lukashenko's regime and push for democratic reforms in Belarus. By targeting the ruling elite and their financial interests, the EU aims to undermine their power and force them to reconsider their oppressive policies. Moreover, the EU's sanctions serve as a symbol of solidarity with the Belarusian people and their struggle for freedom and democracy.

However, the effectiveness of these sanctions has been a subject of debate among historians. While they have succeeded in isolating Lukashenko's regime from the international community to some extent, they have also inadvertently contributed to the consolidation of his power. The sanctions have made Belarus more dependent on Russia, as Lukashenko sought support from his eastern neighbor in the face of Western pressure. This has allowed Russia to exert greater influence over Belarus and further undermine its sovereignty.

Furthermore, the EU's diplomatic pressure has had limited success in bringing about tangible changes in Belarus. Lukashenko's regime has proven resilient and has managed to maintain its grip on power despite the international condemnation. The lack of a unified and coordinated response from the EU member states has also hindered the effectiveness of these measures.

In conclusion, European Union sanctions and diplomatic pressure have been crucial in shaping the dynamics of Alexander Lukashenko's dictatorship in Belarus. While they have symbolized the EU's support for democracy and human rights, their impact on bringing about meaningful change has been limited. The future of Belarus without Lukashenko remains uncertain, and it is essential for historians to analyze the complexity of these measures and their long-term implications for the country's relations with the EU and neighboring countries.

Role of international organizations in condemning Lukashenko's regime

The authoritarian rule of Alexander Lukashenko in Belarus has attracted significant attention from international organizations. These organizations play a crucial role in condemning Lukashenko's regime and advocating for human rights, democracy, and the rule of law. Their efforts are aimed at exposing the oppressive nature of Lukashenko's rule and pressuring the Belarusian government to respect basic freedoms and democratic principles.

International organizations such as the United Nations, European Union, and various human rights groups have consistently criticized Lukashenko's regime for its suppression of political dissent, human rights violations, and lack of media freedom. These organizations have been vocal in their condemnation of the regime's tactics, including arbitrary arrests, torture, and restrictions on freedom of speech and assembly.

The United Nations has been at the forefront of the international response to Lukashenko's dictatorship. Through its human rights bodies, such as the Human Rights Council and the Office of the High Commissioner for Human Rights, the UN has been actively monitoring the human rights situation in Belarus. It has issued numerous reports highlighting the violations committed by Lukashenko's regime and calling for accountability.

Similarly, the European Union has taken a strong stance against Lukashenko's regime. It has imposed targeted sanctions on Belarusian officials involved in human rights abuses and electoral fraud. The EU has also provided support to civil society organizations in Belarus, offering financial assistance and training to promote democracy and human rights.

Human rights groups, such as Amnesty International and Human Rights Watch, have conducted extensive research and documented the human rights violations under Lukashenko's regime. They have raised awareness about the situation in Belarus through reports, campaigns, and advocacy efforts. These organizations have also been instrumental in mobilizing international support for the Belarusian opposition movements and providing assistance to those affected by the regime's repression.

The condemnation of Lukashenko's regime by international organizations has not only brought global attention to the human rights abuses in Belarus but has also put pressure on the regime to change its behavior. The involvement of these organizations has helped to strengthen the voices of the Belarusian people and their struggle for democracy and freedom.

In conclusion, international organizations have played a crucial role in condemning Lukashenko's regime and advocating for human rights, democracy, and the rule of law in Belarus. Their efforts have brought global attention to the human rights abuses and helped to mobilize support for the Belarusian opposition movements. The condemnation by these organizations has put pressure on the regime to respect basic freedoms and democratic principles, and their involvement has been instrumental in the fight for a better future for Belarus.

Support for Belarusian civil society and pro-democracy movements

Belarus, under the iron rule of Alexander Lukashenko, has been a country where civil society and pro-democracy movements have faced relentless challenges. Lukashenko's regime has consistently suppressed dissent and stifled any opposition, leaving little room for the growth and development of civil society. However, despite these obstacles, Belarusian civil society and pro-democracy movements have demonstrated resilience and determination in their fight for a free and democratic Belarus.

One of the key factors that have contributed to the survival and growth of civil society in Belarus is the unwavering support from various international organizations and governments. These entities have recognized the importance of supporting civil society and pro-democracy movements in Belarus and have provided financial assistance, resources, and expertise to help them navigate the oppressive environment.

International NGOs and human rights organizations have played a crucial role in highlighting the human rights violations and political repression under Lukashenko's regime. By documenting and publicizing these abuses, they have raised awareness and garnered international support for the Belarusian civil society. Their advocacy efforts have put pressure on the Belarusian government and created a platform for the voices of the oppressed to be heard.

Governments of democratic nations have also extended their support to Belarusian civil society. They have imposed sanctions on Lukashenko's regime, targeting key individuals and entities responsible for human rights abuses and political repression. These sanctions not only serve as a form of punishment but also provide moral and material support to the Belarusian civil society by demonstrating solidarity with their struggle.

Furthermore, neighboring countries, particularly those in the European Union, have played a crucial role in supporting Belarusian civil society. They have provided platforms for Belarusian activists and opposition leaders to voice their concerns and have offered refuge to those fleeing persecution. In addition, the European Union has implemented programs that promote the development of civil society in Belarus, providing funding and technical assistance to strengthen their capacity and resilience.

The support for Belarusian civil society and pro-democracy movements has not only provided them with much-needed resources but has also given them a sense of hope and encouragement. It has shown them that they are not alone in their fight and that the international community stands with them.

While the challenges facing Belarusian civil society remain formidable, the support they have received has enabled them to continue their struggle for a free and democratic Belarus. The international community's commitment to supporting civil society and pro-democracy movements in Belarus is crucial in ensuring that their voices are heard and that they can work towards a brighter future for their country.

Effectiveness of international efforts in promoting change

Throughout the history of Alexander Lukashenko's reign as Europe's longest ruling dictator, numerous international efforts have been made to promote change in Belarus. From economic policies to human rights violations and suppression of political dissent, the international community has played a crucial role in addressing these issues and advocating for a more democratic and free Belarus.

One of the key areas where international efforts have been focused is Alexander Lukashenko's economic policies and their impact on Belarus. The dictator's policies have led to a stagnant economy, rampant corruption, and a lack of foreign investment. In response, international organizations such as the International Monetary Fund (IMF) and the European Bank for Reconstruction and Development (EBRD) have provided financial assistance and implemented economic reforms to stimulate growth and improve the living standards of the Belarusian people.

Another crucial aspect that has garnered international attention is the human rights violations under Lukashenko's regime. Organizations like Human Rights Watch, Amnesty International, and the United Nations Human Rights Council have consistently documented and condemned the suppression of political dissent, arbitrary arrests, torture, and restrictions on freedom of speech in Belarus. These reports have not only raised awareness but have also put pressure on the regime to adhere to international human rights standards.

In addition, the international response to Lukashenko's dictatorship has been significant. The European Union (EU), United States, and other countries have imposed targeted sanctions on key individuals within the regime, including travel bans and asset freezes. These measures aim to isolate Lukashenko's government and send a clear message that his actions are unacceptable. Furthermore, international forums and diplomatic channels have been utilized to engage in dialogue and negotiations to push for democratic reforms in Belarus.

Despite these efforts, Lukashenko's control over the media and freedom of speech remains a major challenge. The regime tightly controls the information flow and suppresses independent media outlets, making it difficult for the international community to effectively counter the propaganda machinery. However, international media organizations, such as Reporters Without Borders, have continuously shed light on the situation and provided a platform for Belarusian journalists and activists to tell their stories.

The Belarusian opposition movements have been at the forefront of the struggle against Lukashenko's rule, and the international community has shown solidarity and support for their cause. Opposition leaders, activists, and dissidents have been provided with platforms to raise awareness about the human rights abuses and advocate for democratic change. International organizations like the European Network of Election Monitoring Organizations (ENEMO) have also played a crucial role in monitoring elections in Belarus and reporting on irregularities.

Looking ahead, the future of Belarus without Lukashenko remains uncertain. The international community must continue its efforts to promote change and support democratic forces within the country. It is crucial for historians to study and analyze the effectiveness of international efforts in order to learn from past experiences and develop more effective strategies in promoting democracy and human rights not only in Belarus but also in other authoritarian regimes around the world.

Chapter 9: Alexander Lukashenko's Influence on Belarusian Culture and Arts

State control over cultural institutions and censorship

In the realm of state control over cultural institutions and censorship, Alexander Lukashenko's regime in Belarus has established a tight grip on the country's creative sphere. This subchapter delves into the mechanisms employed by Europe's longest ruling dictator to maintain control over cultural expression and suppress dissenting voices.

Lukashenko's authoritarian regime has systematically utilized state control over cultural institutions as a means of promoting its own narrative and stifling any form of opposition. The Ministry of Culture, under direct government influence, exercises extensive control over the arts, including theater, literature, and visual arts. By appointing loyalists to key positions within these institutions, Lukashenko ensures that only content aligned with his regime's ideology is produced and showcased.

Censorship plays a pivotal role in Lukashenko's strategy of maintaining control over cultural expression. The regime tightly monitors and censors media, including newspapers, television, and online platforms. Any content deemed critical or dissenting is swiftly removed or suppressed. This has resulted in a highly restricted media environment, with journalists and media organizations facing severe consequences for reporting on sensitive topics or expressing viewpoints contrary to the regime's narrative.

Lukashenko's control over cultural institutions and censorship has had a profound impact on Belarusian society. The arts, which traditionally serve as a platform for free expression and reflection, have been reduced to mere propaganda tools. Artists and intellectuals who dare to challenge the status quo face persecution, including imprisonment and exile. As a result, many talented individuals have been forced into self-censorship or have chosen to leave the country in search of greater artistic freedom.

The international community has been vocal in condemning Lukashenko's state control over cultural institutions and censorship. Human rights organizations and foreign governments have consistently raised concerns about the suppression of artistic expression and the violation of freedom of speech in Belarus. However, Lukashenko's regime has remained defiant, dismissing such criticism as interference in the country's internal affairs.

As historians, it is imperative that we document and analyze the extent to which Alexander Lukashenko's regime has exerted control over cultural institutions and stifled freedom of expression. By shedding light on these repressive measures, we contribute to a better understanding of the impact of dictatorship on cultural and artistic development. Furthermore, our work serves as a reminder of the importance of preserving and protecting artistic freedom as a fundamental human right.

Promotion of state-sanctioned cultural narratives

One of the key tools utilized by Alexander Lukashenko to solidify his rule over Belarus is the promotion of state-sanctioned cultural narratives. By controlling the cultural landscape of the country, Lukashenko has been able to shape and mold the collective consciousness of the Belarusian people, ensuring their loyalty and compliance with his regime.

Under Lukashenko's regime, the promotion of state-sanctioned cultural narratives has been pervasive and all-encompassing. From schools and universities to the media and arts, every aspect of Belarusian society has been subjected to a carefully curated narrative that serves the interests of the ruling regime. This narrative glorifies Lukashenko as a strong and wise leader, portraying him as the savior of the nation and the only one capable of protecting Belarus from external threats.

One of the primary methods employed by Lukashenko to promote this narrative is through the control of the media and freedom of speech in Belarus. Independent media outlets are suppressed and censored, leaving only government-controlled media to disseminate the regime's propaganda. Any dissenting voices or alternative viewpoints are swiftly silenced, further reinforcing the state-sanctioned narrative.

Another avenue through which Lukashenko has promoted his cultural narrative is through his control over the education system. Schools and universities are used as tools for indoctrination, with textbooks and curriculum designed to instill loyalty and obedience to the regime. History is rewritten to fit the narrative, with Lukashenko's rule portrayed as a period of stability and prosperity, while any mention of opposition movements or human rights violations is conveniently omitted.

The impact of this promotion of state-sanctioned cultural narratives on Belarusian society cannot be overstated. It has created a population that is largely unaware of the true extent of Lukashenko's authoritarian rule and the human rights abuses committed under his regime. It has stifled dissent and opposition, leaving the Belarusian people divided and afraid to speak out against the regime.

As historians, it is crucial that we uncover and expose the truth behind Lukashenko's promotion of state-sanctioned cultural narratives. By shedding light on the mechanisms and tactics employed by the regime, we can contribute to a more comprehensive understanding of Lukashenko's rule and its implications for Belarus. Only through knowledge and awareness can we hope to challenge and dismantle the oppressive cultural narratives that have been imposed upon the Belarusian people.

Exile and repression of artists and intellectuals

In the annals of Alexander Lukashenko's oppressive regime, the plight of artists and intellectuals stands as a haunting testament to the lengths he would go to stifle dissent and silence any form of opposition. From the early days of his presidency, Lukashenko's iron grip on power extended into the realms of culture and intellect, leaving a lasting impact on Belarusian society.

Under Lukashenko's rule, artists and intellectuals found themselves in the crosshairs of state repression. Many prominent figures in the arts and academia were forced into exile, their voices effectively silenced and their contributions to Belarusian culture lost to the world. This systematic targeting of creative minds was a calculated move to eliminate any form of critical thinking and alternative narratives that could challenge Lukashenko's regime.

The methods employed to suppress artists and intellectuals were multifaceted. The regime used a combination of legal harassment, intimidation, and censorship to exert control over the creative sphere. Dissenting voices were met with threats of imprisonment or physical harm, leading many artists and intellectuals to self-censor or flee the country in fear for their safety.

The impact of this exile and repression on Belarusian culture cannot be overstated. The loss of these creative minds has led to a stifling of artistic expression, leaving a void in the cultural landscape of Belarus. The absence of critical voices has allowed Lukashenko's regime to shape the narrative and control the discourse, further entrenching his dictatorship.

However, despite these oppressive measures, the resilience of Belarusian artists and intellectuals cannot be overlooked. Even in exile, they continue to fight for their right to express themselves and shed light on the realities of Lukashenko's rule. Their work serves as a powerful testament to the strength of the human spirit and the indomitable nature of creativity in the face of adversity.

As historians, it is our duty to document and analyze the exile and repression of artists and intellectuals under Lukashenko's regime. By shedding light on this dark chapter in Belarusian history, we contribute to the understanding of the devastating impact of dictatorship on cultural and intellectual life. It is through our collective efforts that we can ensure that the voices of the silenced are heard, and the legacy of Lukashenko's repression is never forgotten.

Resilience and underground cultural movements

Resilience and underground cultural movements have played a significant role in the history of Belarus under the rule of Alexander Lukashenko, Europe's longest ruling dictator. This subchapter aims to explore the impact of Lukashenko's regime on the underground cultural movements in Belarus, highlighting the resilience and determination of the Belarusian people to express their artistic and cultural identity despite suppression.

Lukashenko's regime has consistently sought to control and manipulate the cultural landscape of Belarus, using it as a tool to further his political agenda and maintain his grip on power. The state-controlled media and censorship have been instrumental in suppressing dissent and promoting a narrative that aligns with Lukashenko's regime. However, underground cultural movements have emerged as a response to this repression, serving as a platform for artists, writers, musicians, and performers to express their opposition and challenge the status quo.

Despite facing constant surveillance, harassment, and intimidation from the state, these underground cultural movements have demonstrated incredible resilience and creativity in finding ways to express their dissent. They have utilized alternative spaces, such as abandoned buildings, private homes, and secret venues, to organize performances, exhibitions, and gatherings that celebrate freedom of expression and challenge the oppressive regime.

The Belarusian underground cultural movements have adopted various forms, including punk rock, street art, literature, and theater, to convey their messages of resistance. These artistic expressions have become powerful tools to unite like-minded individuals, foster solidarity, and raise awareness about the human rights violations and political repression under Lukashenko's rule.

However, the road to resilience has not been easy for these underground movements. Many artists and activists have faced persecution, arbitrary arrests, and imprisonment for their involvement in these movements. Despite these challenges, they continue to push boundaries, inspire others, and keep the spirit of resistance alive.

The international community has also recognized the significance of these underground cultural movements in Belarus. Artists and activists have received support and recognition from international organizations, cultural institutions, and human rights groups, amplifying their voices and providing them with a global platform to showcase their work.

As historians, it is crucial to acknowledge the resilience and impact of underground cultural movements in the face of Lukashenko's repressive regime. By highlighting their struggles, achievements, and contributions to the Belarusian cultural landscape, we shed light on the power of art and creativity in challenging authoritarian rule. These movements pave the way for a future Belarus that is free, democratic, and thriving in its cultural diversity.

Chapter 10: Alexander Lukashenko's Legacy and the Future of Belarus Without Him

Assessment of Lukashenko's impact on Belarusian society and politics

Introduction:

Alexander Lukashenko, Europe's longest ruling dictator, has left an indelible mark on Belarusian society and politics since assuming power in 1994. This subchapter aims to delve into the multifaceted aspects of Lukashenko's reign, exploring his economic policies, suppression of political dissent, human rights violations, relationship with Russia, control over the media, opposition movements, international response, influence on Belarusian culture, his legacy, and foreign policy implications. By analyzing these dimensions, historians can gain a comprehensive understanding of Lukashenko's impact on Belarus.

Economic Policies and their Impact on Belarus:

Lukashenko's economic policies have been characterized by state intervention, protectionism, and a focus on heavy industry. While initially successful, these policies have led to stagnation, inefficiency, and a lack of diversification in the Belarusian economy. Historians must assess the long-term consequences of these policies for Belarus and its people.

Suppression of Political Dissent and Human Rights Violations:

Under Lukashenko's regime, political dissent has been systematically suppressed. Opposition leaders, activists, and journalists have faced intimidation, arbitrary arrests, and unfair trials. Human rights violations, including torture and censorship, have been rampant. Historians must examine the extent of these violations and their impact on Belarusian society.

Relationship with Russia and Implications for Belarus:

Lukashenko's close ties with Russia have shaped Belarus' foreign policy and domestic affairs. Historians should explore the implications of this alliance on Belarus' sovereignty, political autonomy, and economic dependence. Additionally, the impact of Lukashenko's pro-Russian stance on Belarus' relations with the EU and neighboring countries must be analyzed.

Control over Media and Freedom of Speech:

Lukashenko has maintained strict control over the media, suppressing any dissenting voices and limiting freedom of speech. Historians must assess the impact of this control on the dissemination of information, public opinion, and the ability of Belarusian society to express itself freely.

Opposition Movements and Struggle against Lukashenko's Rule:

Despite severe repression, Belarusian opposition movements have persisted in their struggle against Lukashenko's rule. Historians must examine the tactics, strategies, and challenges faced by these movements, as well as the impact they have had on Belarusian society and politics.

International Response to Lukashenko's Dictatorship:

The international community has responded to Lukashenko's dictatorship with varying degrees of condemnation and sanctions. Historians should analyze the effectiveness of these responses and their impact on Lukashenko's regime.

Influence on Belarusian Culture and Arts:

Lukashenko's regime has exerted control over Belarusian culture and arts, promoting a state-approved narrative and stifling dissenting voices. Historians must assess the impact of this control on the development of Belarusian culture and artistic expression.

Legacy and the Future of Belarus without Lukashenko:

As Lukashenko's grip on power appears to be weakening, historians must contemplate the potential consequences of his departure on Belarusian society and politics. What will be Lukashenko's lasting legacy, and how will it shape the future of Belarus?

Foreign Policy and its Impact on Belarus' Relations:

Lukashenko's foreign policy, particularly his dealings with the EU and neighboring countries, has had a significant impact on Belarus' international standing. Historians should evaluate the consequences of Lukashenko's foreign policy choices on Belarus' relations and potential future trajectories.

Conclusion:

Assessing Lukashenko's impact on Belarusian society and politics requires a comprehensive analysis of his economic policies, suppression of dissent, human rights violations, relationship with Russia, control over the media, opposition movements, international response, cultural influence, legacy, and foreign policy. By scrutinizing these dimensions, historians can contribute to a deeper understanding of Lukashenko's rule and its far-reaching consequences for Belarus.

Transition of power and potential scenarios for the post-Lukashenko era

As historians, it is our duty to analyze and anticipate the potential scenarios that may unfold in the post-Lukashenko era in Belarus. Alexander Lukashenko, who holds the record for Europe's longest ruling dictator, has shaped the nation's politics, economy, and society for over two decades. However, the winds of change are blowing, and it is essential to examine the possible outcomes of a transition of power in Belarus.

One potential scenario is a smooth and peaceful transition, where a new leader emerges through democratic means. This could pave the way for much-needed reforms and the restoration of human rights and civil liberties. The economic policies implemented by Lukashenko have had a significant impact on Belarus, and a new administration may focus on diversifying the economy, reducing state control, and attracting foreign investment.

On the other hand, a more turbulent scenario may involve a power struggle among various factions within the government or opposition movements. Belarusian society has long struggled under Lukashenko's suppression of political dissent, and this scenario could lead to a period of instability and uncertainty. The international community would closely monitor the situation, as neighboring countries and the European Union have a vested interest in the stability of Belarus.

Another scenario worth considering is the influence of Russia on the transition of power in Belarus. Lukashenko's relationship with Russia has been complex, with Belarus heavily dependent on its neighbor for economic and political support. In the post-Lukashenko era, the question arises whether Russia will continue to exert influence or if Belarus will strive for greater autonomy and closer ties with the European Union.

Furthermore, the control over the media and freedom of speech in Belarus has been a defining characteristic of Lukashenko's regime. A post-Lukashenko era could witness a newfound openness and freedom for journalists, artists, and intellectuals, leading to a flourishing of Belarusian culture and arts.

Ultimately, the legacy of Alexander Lukashenko and the future of Belarus without him are intertwined. The international response to his dictatorship will play a crucial role in shaping the nation's future. It is essential for historians to closely examine the impact of Lukashenko's rule on Belarusian society and assess the possibilities and challenges that lie ahead in the post-Lukashenko era.

Challenges and opportunities for democratic reforms

Introduction:

The subchapter "Challenges and Opportunities for Democratic Reforms" delves into the complex issues surrounding Alexander Lukashenko's regime and the potential for democratic reforms in Belarus. This section aims to provide historians with an in-depth analysis of the obstacles faced by Belarusians seeking democratic change, as well as the potential opportunities that may arise in the future.

Challenges to Democratic Reforms:

Lukashenko's Economic Policies: One of the major challenges impeding democratic reforms in Belarus is the economic policies implemented by Lukashenko. His state-centric economic model, characterized by heavy state intervention, has hindered the development of a vibrant private sector, stifled entrepreneurship, and perpetuated a reliance on Russia.

Suppression of Political Dissent: Another significant challenge lies in Lukashenko's relentless suppression of political dissent. Through tactics such as arbitrary arrests, imprisonments, and harassment of opposition leaders, Lukashenko has effectively silenced dissenting voices and weakened the prospects for democratic reforms.

Human Rights Violations: The persistent human rights violations under Lukashenko's regime pose a significant challenge to democratic reforms. Reports of torture, arbitrary detentions, and restrictions on freedom of expression and assembly continue to tarnish Belarus' international reputation and hinder efforts to achieve democratic change.

Media Control and Freedom of Speech: Lukashenko's tight grip over the media and limited freedom of speech further exacerbate the challenges faced by those advocating for democratic reforms. Independent media outlets face censorship and harassment, limiting access to unbiased information and hindering the formation of a well-informed citizenry.

Opportunities for Democratic Reforms:

Belarusian Opposition Movements: Despite facing numerous challenges, Belarusian opposition movements have shown resilience and determination in their struggle against Lukashenko's rule. These movements, such as the Belarusian National Congress and the United Civic Party, present opportunities for democratic reforms through their grassroots mobilization and advocacy for human rights.

International Response: The international response to Lukashenko's dictatorship presents another potential opportunity for democratic reforms. Increased condemnation and pressure from the international community, including economic sanctions, can have a significant impact on Lukashenko's regime and potentially create openings for democratic changes.

Legacy and the Future of Belarus: As Lukashenko's regime nears its end, there is an opportunity to shape the future of Belarus. The legacy left behind by Europe's longest ruling dictator can serve as a catalyst for democratic reforms, fostering a renewed sense of national identity and a desire for change among Belarusians.

Conclusion:

The subchapter "Challenges and Opportunities for Democratic Reforms" highlights the multifaceted obstacles faced by Belarusians seeking democratic change, from Lukashenko's economic policies and suppression of political dissent to human rights violations and media control. However, it also identifies potential opportunities for democratic reforms, including the resilience of opposition movements, the international response to Lukashenko's regime, and the potential for a renewed national identity. By understanding these challenges and opportunities, historians can gain a comprehensive understanding of the complex dynamics surrounding Alexander Lukashenko's dictatorship and its implications for the future of Belarus.

Prospects for Belarus' integration into the European community

As historians delve into the legacy of Alexander Lukashenko, one of the key aspects that demands attention is the prospects for Belarus' integration into the European community. Lukashenko's authoritarian rule has long hindered the nation's progress towards becoming a part of the European Union (EU) and establishing closer ties with neighboring countries. However, recent developments and shifting dynamics have opened up possibilities for change.

Lukashenko's economic policies have played a significant role in Belarus' isolation from Europe. His emphasis on state control and disregard for market principles has resulted in a stagnant economy, marked by inefficiency and corruption. The EU has repeatedly stressed the importance of economic reforms as a prerequisite for Belarus' integration. Nevertheless, recent economic liberalization measures, such as the establishment of the High Technologies Park and the increase in foreign investment, indicate a potential shift towards a more market-oriented approach.

Another major obstacle to Belarus' integration into the European community is Lukashenko's suppression of political dissent. His regime has been notorious for human rights violations and the suppression of opposition movements. This has strained relations with the EU, which has consistently condemned such actions. However, recent developments, including the release of political prisoners and the easing of restrictions on civil society organizations, have raised hopes for a more inclusive political environment.

Lukashenko's relationship with Russia also significantly impacts Belarus' integration prospects. Historically, he has maintained close ties with Russia, relying on economic and political support from Moscow. This has often complicated Belarus' relations with the EU, as the West has been wary of Lukashenko's alignment with Russia. However, recent geopolitical shifts and Lukashenko's efforts to diversify Belarus' foreign policy have opened up opportunities for a more balanced approach, fostering closer ties with both the EU and neighboring countries.

Furthermore, Lukashenko's control over the media and freedom of speech in Belarus has been a major concern for the European community. The regime's tight grip on information dissemination has limited the flow of independent news and stifled freedom of expression. However, recent developments, such as the emergence of online platforms and increased access to alternative sources of information, have provided a glimmer of hope for a more open media environment.

In conclusion, while Alexander Lukashenko's long-standing dictatorship has impeded Belarus' integration into the European community, recent developments offer a glimpse of potential change. Economic reforms, the easing of political restrictions, and a more balanced foreign policy approach all contribute to the prospects for Belarus' integration. As historians analyze Lukashenko's rule, they must closely examine these developments and their implications for the future of Belarus, shedding light on the possibilities that lie ahead.

Chapter 11: Alexander Lukashenko's Foreign Policy and Its Impact on Belarus' Relations with the EU and Neighboring Countries

Lukashenko's balancing act between East and West

In the complex geopolitical landscape of Eastern Europe, Alexander Lukashenko, Europe's longest ruling dictator, has adeptly navigated a delicate balancing act between East and West. Throughout his tenure, Lukashenko has skillfully maintained a strategic equilibrium between the interests of Russia and those of the European Union and neighboring countries.

Lukashenko's economic policies have played a significant role in this balancing act. Despite his authoritarian rule, he implemented certain market-oriented reforms that attracted Western investment and fostered economic growth, thereby appeasing Western powers. However, these reforms were carefully calibrated to avoid relinquishing too much control, ensuring that his grip on power remained intact.

Simultaneously, Lukashenko has maintained a close relationship with Russia, recognizing its economic and political influence in the region. Belarus has long relied on Russian support, particularly in the form of energy subsidies and trade agreements. Lukashenko has skillfully leveraged this dependence to extract concessions from Moscow, ensuring Belarus maintains a degree of autonomy within the Russian sphere of influence.

This balancing act has not come without costs, particularly in terms of human rights and political dissent. Lukashenko's regime has been characterized by widespread suppression of political opposition and human rights violations. Dissenters, journalists, and activists have faced harassment, imprisonment, and even disappearances. The control Lukashenko exercises over the media and freedom of speech has further stifled opposition voices and perpetuated his rule.

Belarusian opposition movements have emerged in response to Lukashenko's autocratic regime, striving to challenge his rule and advocate for democratic reforms. These movements have faced significant obstacles, with their leaders often facing imprisonment or exile. However, they continue to persist, fueled by a desire for change and the hope for a Belarus free from the grip of Lukashenko's dictatorship.

Internationally, Lukashenko's regime has drawn criticism and condemnation for its human rights abuses. However, the response from the international community has been mixed, with some countries imposing sanctions and others maintaining diplomatic engagement. The delicate geopolitical balance in the region, coupled with Lukashenko's realpolitik approach, has influenced how the international community navigates its relationship with Belarus.

As Lukashenko's rule approaches its end, questions arise regarding his legacy and the future of Belarus without him. His influence on Belarusian culture and arts cannot be understated, with his regime promoting a narrative of national identity that has shaped the country's artistic landscape. However, his legacy is marred by human rights abuses and political repression, leaving a complex and contentious legacy for future generations to grapple with.

The future of Belarus without Lukashenko remains uncertain. His foreign policy, which has carefully balanced relations with both the EU and Russia, will undoubtedly impact Belarus' future relations with these actors. As the country moves forward, it will face the challenge of navigating its place in the larger European context, determining its allegiances, and shaping its own destiny.

In conclusion, Alexander Lukashenko's balancing act between East and West has been a defining feature of his rule. Through skillful economic policies, control over the media, suppression of political dissent, and careful diplomacy, he has maintained a delicate equilibrium between the interests of Russia and the Western world. As his reign nears its end, the consequences of this balancing act will shape the future of Belarus and its place in the global order.

Cooperation and conflicts with neighboring countries

Throughout his lengthy rule, Alexander Lukashenko has faced both cooperation and conflicts with neighboring countries, shaping the trajectory of Belarus' foreign policy. This subchapter explores the intricacies of these relationships, shedding light on the dynamics between Lukashenko's regime and its neighbors.

Belarus, a landlocked country in Eastern Europe, shares borders with several nations, including Russia, Ukraine, Poland, Lithuania, and Latvia. Lukashenko's relationship with Russia has been a focal point of Belarus' foreign policy, with Moscow being a key ally and economic partner. Lukashenko has often utilized this alliance to secure economic support and maintain his grip on power. However, this cooperation has not been without conflicts, as Russia has occasionally exerted pressure on Lukashenko to advance its own interests.

On the other hand, Lukashenko's relationship with Ukraine has been marked by tension and conflicts. The annexation of Crimea by Russia and the ongoing conflict in Eastern Ukraine have strained the bilateral ties between the two countries. Lukashenko has tried to position Belarus as a mediator in the conflict, but his efforts have often been met with skepticism from the international community.

Belarus' relations with its European neighbors, particularly Poland and Lithuania, have been mixed. While Lukashenko has sought economic cooperation with these countries, his authoritarian rule and human rights violations have strained diplomatic ties. The European Union has imposed sanctions on Belarus, and Lukashenko's repressive measures against political dissent have further deepened the divide.

Conflicts have also arisen with neighboring countries over territorial disputes and energy resources. For instance, the construction of the Astravets nuclear power plant near the Lithuanian border has sparked concerns about safety and environmental impact. Lukashenko's dismissive approach to these concerns has strained Belarus' relations with its Baltic neighbor.

In summary, Lukashenko's rule has witnessed both cooperation and conflicts with neighboring countries. While his alliance with Russia has been crucial for Belarus' economic stability, it has also subjected the country to Russian influence. Lukashenko's relationships with Ukraine, Poland, Lithuania, and other European neighbors have been marred by conflicts arising from his authoritarian rule, human rights violations, and territorial disputes. These dynamics have significantly shaped Belarus' foreign policy and continue to impact its relations with the EU and neighboring countries.

EU-Belarus relations under Lukashenko's rule

The relationship between the European Union (EU) and Belarus under the authoritarian regime of Alexander Lukashenko has been marked by tension, isolation, and limited cooperation. Lukashenko, Europe's longest-ruling dictator, has maintained a firm grip on power since 1994, defying democratic norms and suppressing political dissent. This subchapter aims to provide a comprehensive analysis of the dynamics surrounding EU-Belarus relations during Lukashenko's rule, shedding light on the impact of his policies on Belarus and the wider region.

Lukashenko's economic policies have played a crucial role in shaping EU-Belarus relations. His heavy-handed approach to the economy, characterized by state control and limited market liberalization, has hindered economic growth and deterred foreign investment. The EU, historically supportive of economic reforms and market-oriented policies, has expressed concerns about Belarus' lack of progress in this regard, leading to strained relations between the two parties.

Furthermore, Lukashenko's suppression of political dissent and human rights violations have garnered international condemnation. The EU has consistently criticized his regime for its disregard for democratic principles, leading to the imposition of targeted sanctions against Belarusian officials. These measures, however, have had limited impact in changing Lukashenko's behavior, highlighting the complex nature of EU-Belarus relations.

Lukashenko's close ties with Russia have further complicated EU-Belarus relations. Belarus, heavily reliant on Russian economic support, has become a strategic ally for Moscow. This alignment with Russia has raised concerns within the EU, as it perceives Lukashenko's regime as a potential threat to regional stability and a pawn in Russia's geopolitical maneuvers.

The control over the media and freedom of speech in Belarus has also been a key point of contention between the EU and Lukashenko's regime. Independent media outlets have faced repression and censorship, limiting the flow of information and stifling public discourse. The EU has consistently called for media freedom and press independence in Belarus, but Lukashenko's tight grip on the media landscape has made progress in this area challenging.

Despite the repressive environment, Belarusian opposition movements have persistently struggled against Lukashenko's rule, often facing persecution and imprisonment. The EU has provided financial and moral support to these movements, aiming to promote democracy and human rights in Belarus. However, the effectiveness of these efforts has been limited, as Lukashenko's regime has proven resilient and adept at suppressing dissent.

Internationally, the response to Lukashenko's dictatorship has been mixed. While the EU and the United States have imposed targeted sanctions, Russia and some neighboring countries have continued to support Lukashenko's regime. This divergence of approaches has further complicated EU-Belarus relations and hindered the possibility of a collective response to the ongoing political crisis in Belarus.

Looking towards the future, the question of Lukashenko's legacy and the future of Belarus without him looms large. As Europe's longest-ruling dictator, Lukashenko's departure from power is likely to have a profound impact on the country's political landscape, regional dynamics, and EU-Belarus relations. The EU, along with other international actors, will need to carefully navigate this transition and support Belarus in its path towards democracy and stability.

In conclusion, EU-Belarus relations under Lukashenko's rule have been characterized by tension, limited cooperation, and concerns over human rights violations and democratic backsliding. Lukashenko's economic policies, suppression of political dissent, close ties with Russia, control over the media, and repression of opposition movements have all played a role in shaping the dynamics between the EU and Belarus. As Lukashenko's regime faces mounting challenges and calls for change grow louder, the future of EU-Belarus relations remains uncertain, but the need for a strategic and principled approach from the EU is more crucial than ever.

Future implications for Belarus' geopolitical position

The future implications for Belarus' geopolitical position are a topic of great interest and concern for historians studying Alexander Lukashenko's reign as Europe's longest ruling dictator. As his grip on power continues to tighten, it is crucial to examine the potential consequences of his leadership for the country's geopolitical standing.

Lukashenko's economic policies have had a profound impact on Belarus, leading to both positive and negative implications for its geopolitical position. On one hand, his emphasis on state control and protectionist measures has allowed the country to maintain a degree of economic stability and independence. However, this has also hindered economic diversification and modernization, making Belarus heavily dependent on Russia for trade and resources. As a result, the country's geopolitical position is vulnerable to fluctuations in the Russian economy and political dynamics.

Furthermore, Lukashenko's suppression of political dissent and human rights violations have strained Belarus' relations with the European Union and neighboring countries. The international community has consistently condemned Lukashenko's regime for its lack of democracy and human rights abuses. This has resulted in economic sanctions and diplomatic isolation, further limiting Belarus' options for geopolitical alliances and partnerships.

Lukashenko's close relationship with Russia has been a defining feature of Belarus' geopolitical position. While it has provided economic support and security guarantees, it has also led to a loss of sovereignty and dependence on Moscow. As Lukashenko's regime faces increasing pressure from the West, the implications for Belarus' geopolitical position could include greater alignment with Russia and a further distancing from the EU and neighboring countries.

The control over the media and freedom of speech in Belarus has also had significant implications for the country's geopolitical standing. The lack of press freedom and independent media has limited the flow of information and stifled public discourse. This has made it difficult for Belarus to present itself as a democratic and transparent nation on the international stage, undermining its credibility and influence.

Looking ahead, the future of Belarus without Lukashenko remains uncertain. His legacy and the impact of his foreign policy choices will have lasting implications for the country's relations with the EU and neighboring countries. The Belarusian opposition movements, despite facing immense challenges under Lukashenko's rule, offer hope for a more democratic future. Whether Belarus can break free from its geopolitical constraints and forge new alliances will depend on a combination of internal developments and external factors.

In conclusion, the future implications for Belarus' geopolitical position are multifaceted and complex. From economic dependencies to human rights abuses, Lukashenko's reign has shaped the country's standing in the international arena. Understanding these implications is crucial for historians seeking to analyze the historical context and long-term consequences of Europe's longest ruling dictator.

Conclusion: Reflections on Alexander Lukashenko's Longest Ruling Dictatorship in Europe

As we conclude our historical analysis of Alexander Lukashenko's reign as Europe's longest ruling dictator, it becomes evident that his regime has had a profound impact on Belarus and its people. This subchapter aims to provide a reflection on the key aspects of Lukashenko's dictatorship and their implications for the country's past, present, and future.

Throughout his rule, Lukashenko implemented economic policies that prioritized state control and isolationism, resulting in a stagnant economy and limited opportunities for growth. The impact of these policies on Belarus and its people cannot be understated, as they have hindered the country's development and left its citizens struggling to make ends meet.

In addition to his economic policies, Lukashenko's suppression of political dissent has been a hallmark of his regime. The human rights violations committed under his rule have been well-documented, with reports of torture, arbitrary arrests, and intimidation tactics employed against opposition figures and activists. This has created a climate of fear and stifled any meaningful opposition to his rule.

Lukashenko's relationship with Russia has also played a significant role in shaping Belarus' political landscape. His close ties with the Kremlin have allowed him to maintain power and leverage Russian support, but it has come at the cost of Belarus' independence and sovereignty. The implications of this relationship for the future of Belarus remain uncertain, as the country grapples with the challenge of maintaining its identity while being heavily influenced by its neighbor.

Furthermore, Lukashenko's control over the media and freedom of speech in Belarus has severely curtailed the dissemination of alternative viewpoints and stifled public discourse. The lack of independent media has made it difficult for Belarusians to access unbiased information and engage in critical discussions about their country's future.

Despite the challenges faced by the Belarusian opposition movements, they have demonstrated incredible resilience and determination in their struggle against Lukashenko's rule. Their efforts have not gone unnoticed, both domestically and internationally, and have shed light on the need for change in Belarus.

On the international stage, Lukashenko's dictatorship has been met with varying responses. While some countries have condemned his human rights abuses and called for democratic reforms, others have maintained diplomatic relations with his regime. This has raised questions about the effectiveness of international pressure and the willingness of the international community to prioritize human rights over political interests.

Lastly, Lukashenko's influence on Belarusian culture and arts cannot be overlooked. His regime's control over cultural institutions and censorship practices have limited artistic expression and creativity, stifling the potential of Belarusian artists.

As we contemplate Lukashenko's legacy and the future of Belarus without him, it is crucial to consider the impact of his foreign policy and its implications for the country's relations with the EU and neighboring countries. The path forward for Belarus will require a delicate balance between maintaining stability and embracing democratic reforms.

In conclusion, Alexander Lukashenko's longest ruling dictatorship in Europe has left an indelible mark on Belarus and its people. The challenges faced by the country in terms of economic stagnation, political suppression, human rights violations, and limited freedom of speech are significant. As historians, it is our duty to continue monitoring and analyzing the developments in Belarus and to contribute to the discourse surrounding the country's future.